ENVIRONMENTAL PLANNING

1939–1969

Volume II

NATIONAL PARKS AND RECREATION IN THE COUNTRYSIDE

BY

GORDON E. CHERRY

LONDON

HER MAJESTY'S STATIONERY OFFICE

© *Crown copyright 1975*
First published 1975

Government Bookshops

HER MAJESTY'S STATIONERY OFFICE
49 High Holborn, London WC1V 6HB
13a Castle Street, Edinburgh EH2 3AR
41 The Hayes, Cardiff CF1 1JW
Brazennose Street, Manchester M60 8AS
Southey House, Wine Street, Bristol BS1 2BQ
258 Broad Street, Birmingham B1 2HE
80 Chichester Street, Belfast BT1 4JY

*Government publications are also available
through booksellers*

ISBN 0 11 630183 x*

711 ENV
(37638/76)

Printed in England for Her Majesty's Stationery Office by Ebenezer Baylis & Son Ltd
The Trinity Press, Worcester, and London
Dd 289457 K16 7/75

ENVIRONMENTAL PLANNING
1939–1969

VOLUME II

The author has been given full access to official documents. He alone is responsible for the statements made and the views expressed.

CONTENTS

CONTENTS

ACKNOWLEDGMENTS

THE sources for this second volume of the Official History of Environmental Planning have been Government papers and Departmental files. From the Cabinet, papers from the Home Affairs Committee, the Lord Privy Seal's Committee and Cabinet Papers and Conclusions have provided most of the material. From the Departments, files from the Ministry of Town and Country Planning, the Ministry of Housing and Local Government, the Department of Health for Scotland, the Scottish Development Department, the Ministry of Agriculture and Fisheries, and the Treasury have provided complementary information. For the 1949 Act the Secretary's Bill Papers were a useful assembly. For background material it has been necessary to draw on certain published documents, notably Committee Reports published as Command Papers and the Annual Reports of the National Parks Commission. I am grateful to the staff of the Cabinet Office, and the Registry staff and Library staff of the Department of the Environment and the Scottish Development Department for their help in producing these files and records.

I wish to record my sincere thanks to the officials who read and commented on an early draft of this volume; to Mr. C. J. Child and his colleagues in the Historical Section of the Cabinet Office for unfailing support and helpfulness; and to Miss G. R. Vale and Miss L. Campbell for their research assistance. To Professor J. B. Cullingworth I am particularly indebted for his advice and guidance, and the opportunity to engage on this study.

I have been given full access to all documents that I have required, I have quoted freely from them, but the responsibility for selection, interpretation and comment is solely mine.

Gordon E. Cherry
December 1974.

CHAPTER 1

Introduction

THE two related questions of National Parks and recreation in the countryside occupy a prominent place in the development of 20th century land use and environmental planning. In introducing this Official History it is useful first of all to be reminded of this fact: we are dealing with no isolated subject matter, but one which is woven into a much wider context.

Up to the 1920s the scope of town planning had been confined largely to matters of civic art, housing layout and design, the propagandists' lobby for garden cities, and the preparation of a handful of schemes for suburban development.* In the inter-war years this canvas widened, and one of the first additional areas of concern was that of countryside amenity. The early regional planning schemes prepared during the twenties drew attention to the need to preserve land of good landscape value from despoliation by sporadic building development. Moreover, the suburban spread, particularly around London, and the population pressure on land resources in the Home Counties generally, was greatly prejudicing the future of certain areas. Notably these were certain stretches of the Thames valley, the heaths, hills and woodlands of the South East, downland country and coastal areas. The founding of the Council for the Preservation of Rural England in 1926 was evidence of the concern for careful countryside management. The need to provide land for rural recreation was an early element in rudimentary countryside planning, and on a specific matter, as early as 1929 a Government Committee was set up to examine the subject of National Parks and their relevance for Britain.

During the thirties the question of reserving countryside areas for amenity and recreation purposes grew in urgency. At least two related issues combined to create what was essentially a new situation. First there was the need to *ensure* that certain land could be adequately preserved from building development. Voluntary agreements had their place, and the National Trust was a valuable agent in landscape protection, but increasingly it seemed likely that an extension of Government powers was necessary to meet certain

---

* For a general review see Gordon E. Cherry, *The Evolution of British Town Planning*, Leonard Hill Books, 1974.

1

objectives. There was a number of cases to consider. On the one hand there were the extensive areas of fine landscape value, such as Snowdonia and the Lake District. On the other there were the much more localised areas of scenic beauty, particularly in evidence in the South East, products of the accidents of geology and landscape evolution. Furthermore, there was the perceived desirability of containing urban growth, particularly that of London, through the device of a green belt. For land reservations to be made on this scale, a number of developments were necessary: new effective powers of land use control, a resolution of the compensation/betterment problem which had so far bedevilled local authorities' attempts at positive land planning, and a co-ordinated planning administration which harmonised the policies of a variety of public bodies.

The second issue concerned the need to plan for the provision of countryside facilities, bearing in mind the expressed requirements of various sections of the community. Between the wars, new demands were placed on the countryside by urban users. The rise in private car ownership which gave a new-found mobility for a growing number of families was only part of the problem. More importantly, rambling, hiking and cycling became popular activities. The Youth Hostels Association was founded in 1930. The physical health of urban dwellers had been a matter of concern for many years and these outdoor activities were encouraged by a number of organisations. The immediate significance was that great importance was attached to the preservation and improvement of public footpaths and open areas suitable for rambling. The grouse moors of the North, catering for the weekend leisure needs of Lancashire, Yorkshire and Derbyshire, became a focal point of discontent when access was denied or thwarted by landowners, as it frequently was. New powers which guaranteed unrestricted access and freedom of movement were demanded. The Access to Mountains Act, 1939, set out a new form of 'access agreement', but this proved to be an abortive measure.

At the outbreak of the Second World War therefore the issues which fell under the heading of 'National Parks and recreation in the countryside' covered a wide range of problems. Government in the wartime reconstruction period faced these and tackled them. The way it accomplished this task, and the consequences which were set in train, form the substance of this Official History.

During the early and mid-forties insistent pressure from lobbyists encouraged Government to formulate new proposals. The National Parks and Access to Countryside Act, 1949, provided the basis for protecting areas of high landscape value and for developing the recreationalists' use of the countryside. Through the setting up of a Commission it provided a new administrative system for dealing with countryside matters. The Act represented an important plank in the package of the Government's overall planning policies in the late forties; it was in fact part of the new form of centralist land use and environmental planning created at that time. Between 1945 and 1949 there was the Distribution of Industry Act (1945), the New Towns Act (1946), the Town and Country Planning Act (1947) and the 1949 Act. These four pieces of legislation dealt with the questions of location of employment, distribution of population, land use control, planning and related financial provisions, and (finally) National Parks and the countryside.

The years after 1950 may be said to constitute the period of operation of the newly devised system. As in other aspects of planning, the National Parks legislation was administered in the setting of new problems. Few could have anticipated the difficulties that lay ahead. One thorny issue concerned the criteria whereby amenity questions had to be judged in relation to others, particularly national economic interests. The amenity conscious and the National Parks and amenity bodies reacted strongly against any attempts to water down their gains. Decisions in respect of Milford Haven, Trawsfynydd, Fylingdales and other developments were hotly contested. To that extent the inevitable conduct of government in the last 25 years has been born of pragmatism: the pursuance of flexible and evolutionary National Park and countryside policies in the face of dedicated interest groups who maintained their fixed principles to the end. The whole period has been marked by deep differences between the advocates of different policies or administrative systems.

The operation of the new provisions also had to deal with a set of new problems concerned with usage of the countryside. Increasing motorisation of the population, their greater affluence and the advent of weekend leisure for many, put new pressures on the countryside. There was an increasing pressure of demand on resources and facilities and the focus of interest shifted somewhat from National Parks to other areas. Because of continuing absorption of land for building development on an extensive scale, certain land remained heavily at risk, notably coastal belts and land in the vicinity of the larger cities. The emphasis changed from preserving National Parks and their scenic heritage to creating new areas of recreation provision, particularly with a water element, at short distances from the urban areas. The Countryside Act, 1968, made new provisions for access to the countryside and created the country park as a new element in countryside recreation. The National Parks Commission was reconstituted as the Countryside Commission.

This History therefore is important in presenting a study of the issues concerned with an important element of land use and environmental planning over the last 30 years. It is not an isolated story.

It is part of a wider context which itself has a broadly similar pattern: the creation of a new administrative machine and the provision of new powers in response to sectional pressures from the public; its operation in practice; and the build up of new pressures and demands which resulted in the need for a substantial revision of legislation.

The study is instructive in a number of ways. First, it illustrates clearly the various influences on the shaping of Government policy during this period. The role of pressure groups is underlined repeatedly; in a real sense Government policy emerged as a result of outside influence. Not until the actual framing of the legislation did Government come to a clearly defined view as to what it wanted. Until that time it was a case of cautious, but increasingly encouraging reaction to outside pressures. During the forties the insistent and articulate lobby of the Standing Committee on National Parks (of the Councils for the Preservation of Rural England and Wales) was of supreme importance. Their chairman, Sir Norman Birkett, was a key and influential figure with ready access to Government circles. By contrast, the reputation of some of the other bodies was much less. Their readiness to overstate their case and see issues in stark 'black and white' terms was unconvincing, and helped to maintain a view amongst civil servants that the amenity lobby in its extreme expression was tiresome and harmful. Many years before the beginning of the period covered by this History, the Minister of Health's brief for a meeting in March 1933 when he received a deputation from the Amenities Group of Members of the House of Commons contained an apposite comment. It advised him to '. . . interpolate a word as to the advantage of modesty among the advocates of modesty. There is in some quarters too great an inclination to think that their notion of what constitutes amenities is the one certain gospel. Taste is not a matter for dogmatism and, further, the most serious damage that the advocates of amenity can do to their cause is to give to the general public any notion that in their view there is something essentially incompatible between necessary development and amenity.' This was an expression of view which was to be heard more than once during our period.

The study also illustrates the importance of securing a consensus for proposed measures. Countryside legislation was dependent on the foreknowledge that the provisions were broadly acceptable to the main interests involved. The Access to Mountains Act, 1939, was a prime example of this, whereby a Private Member's Bill was shaped according, it was believed, to the interests of those affected; it failed, and was an abortive measure, when it was found that the interests of one party were not satisfied. The 1949 Act received almost universal approval in the stages both prior and subsequent to the publication of the Bill. In Scotland however the situation was substantially different; here a majority view finally had it that a National Parks Act for Scotland was not necessary. In 1967 and 1968 the Countryside Act was widely supported both for Scotland, and England and Wales.

None the less, the admixture of lobby and a general consensus of approach does not necessarily result in legislation. Within government the influence of key figures is still necessary to determine events in one way or another. This History suggests the enormous importance of Lewis Silkin, Minister of Town and Country Planning, 1945–50. In spite of substantial early reservations about the necessity for National Parks legislation in the form that eventually obtained, none the less once intellectually convinced and committed to the proposals, he carried the Bill through in a determined manner. The support of his Departmental officials was not quite as constant or as determined. By contrast to Silkin some succeeding Ministers were not as devoted to maintaining the initiative in National Park affairs.

Government policy is framed against a background of Departmental activity and inter-Departmental consultations. National Parks entered the statute book against a background of uncertainty as to what was the best form of national administration. The history of the Access to Mountains Act, 1939, showed no great desire of any Department to handle the powers, and the question shuttled between the Home Office, the Ministry of Health and the Ministry of Agriculture. The emergence of new Government Departments during the wartime period and the great developments in the field of planning, clearly put National Parks and other land use matters in the court of the Ministry of Town and Country Planning. None the less planning was a relatively new idea and the M.T.C.P. was viewed with caution by some other Departments, notably the Treasury, which had its own role to play in its financial control.

But there were powerful voices by this time for National Park and amenity questions to be handled by another body altogether—one independent of Government. This gave rise to a repetitive debating point: was there a need for a National Parks Commission (or its successor), and if it was created, what role should it have? In the event, a Commission was established, but so hedged about with financial and other restrictions that its future performance was prejudiced. Subsequently the Countryside Commission emerged as a stronger body, but not without its difficulties.

A similar argument over powers and responsibilities extended to the local level. There were deep divisions between those who advocated national control over national parks, and those who saw a greater need for local control. The difference of view has continued up to the present day with passionate feeling about which control is the better guardian of amenity.

Ambivalence about the place of recreation planning in Government (central or local) is indeed a characteristic of our period. There has been a division of responsibility between 'outside, objective' interests and Government Departments. All this has added to uncertainty and fragmentation in this field. The innovation which could be expected from the recruitment of advisory interests has been stifled by an over-riding sense of conflict between Government and Commission, and between national and local interests.

This History is a straightforward one. It traces the steps by which National Parks and related countryside matters entered the Statute Book, and reviews subsequent events in statutory planning over the last 20 years. It is patently not a complete and comprehensive history of recreation planning in the countryside during this period, although it contributes to that wider setting. It is an Official History, with the consequence that the story is written from the point of view of what happened in Government circles—and why. It cannot therefore be a comprehensive history of the time, with the full canvas woven from all the contributory threads. There has been no study of the workings of the National Parks Commission, the Countryside Commission, the Nature Conservancy or any of the lobbies which have so materially contributed to the full story. That research must be conducted at another time.

The chapters unfold as follows. First, I review the emergence and development of the countryside problem before the Second World War, concluding with the abortive Access to Mountains Act, 1939. Particular attention is paid to the Addison Report on National Parks, 1931. Second, I examine the contribution of the advocates for action between 1941 and 1947; the Scott Report, the Dower Report and the Hobhouse Report are covered in some detail. Third, I look at the situation in Scotland up to 1947. I have decided, on balance, that although events in Scotland during this period bore considerable similarity to the situation in England and Wales, sufficient differences emerged, particularly later on, for the Scottish situation to be treated separately throughout. Fourth, I trace the framing and passing of the 1949 Act: the contribution of the influential bodies, reaction to the draft proposals and to the Bill itself. Fifth, I look at the Act in operation in England and Wales during the fifties: when the argument about National Park Boards continued, when the Commission provided views as to the future amendment of the Act, and when new amenity questions in National Park areas focused new concern as to the success of the legislation. Sixth, I describe the steps whereby the legislation was revised, from Arthur Blenkinsop's Bill of 1959 to successive skirmishes concerning a revision of the Act between 1959 and 1964; and then in the context of changing pressures on the countryside, to the proposals for new legislation between 1964 and 1967, to reactions to the Bill (for England and Wales) of 1967 and to the passing of the 1968 Act. Seventh, I review Scottish developments from 1949 to the 1967 Act. The History concludes at 1969, but I offer a final chapter as an overview in which I bring together some main impressions.

This is the second volume of the Official History of Environmental Planning, which was announced by the Prime Minister in December 1969.* The first was concerned with Planning for Reconstruction and dealt with the period of the early and mid-1940s.† The two volumes therefore overlap to some extent and the two themes, National Parks and the Reconstruction Years, are interlinked. Occasional cross references are given in this volume, but beyond these it is necessary to remember that throughout the 1940s proposals for National Park planning had the very important context of developing ideas about, and proposals for, new legislation and the new planning system for post-war Britain.

---

* H.C. Debates, Vol. 793, cols. 411–12, 18 December 1969.
† *Environmental Planning 1939–69*, Vol. I, J. B. Cullingworth, H.M.S.O., 1975.

CHAPTER 2

The Countryside Problem Between the Wars

URING the 1930s the questions concerned with recreation in
the countryside took on a new importance. There were three
main issues which together provided the setting against which
the first period of this History might be seen. First, there was the
growing need to preserve the amenities of the countryside against
urban sprawl and the more unsightly features of uncontrolled urban
development. The difficulties of withstanding the pressures resulting
from the spread of Greater London were especially marked. Second,
there was the concern shown for the country's areas of high landscape value, as in Snowdonia, Cumbria and Scotland. The creation
of National Parks was suggested in order that they might be protected and their facilities enhanced in the wider interests of the
community. Third, there was the need to ensure availability of
access to the countryside, not only through footpaths and bridleways in the immediate vicinity of London and the larger cities
but also to extensive areas of open land for hikers. Attention became
focused on mountain and moorland, particularly in Northern
England.

Preservation of the Countryside

As early as 1926 the Ministry of Health had stressed 'the need
for the preservation of considerable tracts of land against the
modern spread of building development, often of a sprawling kind,
over ever-widening circles of rural land. The saving of cliffs, downland, or other natural features from indiscriminate building invasion
is but one form of the problem, which in its broadest aspect is that
of setting some limit to the merging of town and country, and the
consequent loss of identity of both, by reserving agricultural or other
forms of open belts in the vicinity of towns, not necessarily always or
generally with a view to public acquisition.'[1] As the Ministry was
quick to acknowledge, this was a large problem, 'which, for its full
solution, requires comprehensive schemes for the distribution and
grouping of development over the countryside affected'.[2] It was
gradually realised that partial remedies, appropriate enough as they
were in their local context, were not sufficient. But town and country
planning did not progress sufficiently during the inter-war years for

9

any effective measures to be taken on a comprehensive basis. We had to wait for the new planning powers after the war for this to be possible.

The early advice of the Ministry of Health was for local authorities in their town planning schemes 'to allocate an ample margin of land particularly suitable for building development for that purpose, and to restrict general building development on other land by means of reservations of private open spaces and agricultural belts. It is not desirable that a large amount of such land should be taken out of cultivation and turned into public open space. All that is required is that it should be preserved as open country.'[3] A major problem in pursuing this policy was financial: the owner of the reserved land was entitled to claim compensation. Local authorities were empowered by the Town Planning Act, 1925, to claim betterment from other owners whose land was increased in value owing to the reservation, but only half of the increase in value could be recovered. Because of the considerable claims for compensation which were possible, great reliance was placed on co-operation with land owners who would agree to reserve private open spaces and agricultural belts without submitting claims.

Through a piecemeal process of acquisition by local authorities and voluntary provision by private bodies a number of rural areas were preserved. But there was evidence to suggest that a combination of differences of view between adjoining local authorities, inadequate powers and financial problems was more than sufficient to render countryside schemes on a regional basis an unlikely strategy. We may instance the general scheme developed for the protection and preservation of the South Coast Downs. It began in 1926 when Eastbourne C.B. Council obtained special parliamentary powers to enable them to acquire extensive areas of downs and downlands. By the 1930s[4] the situation was that West Sussex C.C. was preparing a scheme for the downland in the County under powers relinquished to them by the County District Councils, with the exception of Worthing. On the other hand, the East Sussex C.C. promoted a Parliamentary Bill for the preservation of the downland in the County, but the Bill was rejected. Under the Town and Country Planning Act, 1932, the local authorities had made resolutions to prepare schemes covering the whole area. However, adequate preservation involved compensation, and financial burdens were likely to be greater than District Councils could face unaided. To add to the difficulties there were differences of view between Brighton C.B. and the County Council over what the implications of preservation were. Evidence such as this from the South Coast revealed fundamental inadequacies in the piecemeal approach to securing an effective distribution of recreation land. New measures for land planning in the 1940s were sought to remedy these deficiencies.

On the other hand, there were some encouraging signs to record. In the Lake District, for example, a Joint Advisory Planning Committee was established in 1934 by the three County Councils concerned, and it was hoped that unified arrangements might be made for the guidance of development and the preservation of the outstanding characteristics of the area. In the South of England particularly, a number of notable reservations and purchases were made of outstanding countryside or coastline. In many areas the National Trust extended its activities, and it was believed that vendors or donors of land were attracted by assurances of inalienability. As a result of legislation in 1937, authorities ranging in scale from County Councils to Parish Councils could hand over land to the National Trust to be held by them; they could also make contributions to the expenses of acquisition by the Trust of land or buildings.

The whole question of rural planning was in an embryo state, however. In rural areas the object of a local authority was usually to prevent inappropriate development, but to allow any necessary building, while avoiding an unnecessary liability to compensation.[5] The Town and Country Planning Act, 1932, enabled schemes to be made with the object of protecting existing amenities, but it authorised the exclusion of compensation only for strictly limited provisions. Of these, we should note the following three: a provision which limited the number of buildings, one which restricted the manner in which buildings may be used, and one which prohibited or restricted building operations only pending the coming into operation of a General Development Order. Local authorities could include in their schemes a total prohibition of any building, but they were liable to claims of compensation. In order to avoid such claims, local authorities began to devise particular forms of zoning, the intention being to control building over undeveloped areas of the country on the basis of different densities, varying from one house to two acres, to one house to 100 acres.

The effectiveness of local authority planning in rural areas was the context for Sir Kingsley Wood's motion, accepted by the House of Commons on 10 February 1937, 'That this House deplores the destruction of beauty in town and country and the danger to houses of historic or architectural interest, declares that these are matters of national concern, and is of opinion that the Government should take active steps to ascertain whether its existing powers are adequate or whether they require substantial reinforcement.' The Minister of Health (Walter Elliot) asked his Town and Country Planning

11

Advisory Committee, first appointed in 1934,* to consider the matter.

The Committee presented their *Report on the Preservation of the Countryside*[6] in July 1938. They came to the view that existing powers for the preservation of the countryside were adequate if they were firmly administered; none the less they had a number of important suggestions to make. For example they considered that there was a case for making a part of the cost of preserving holiday areas a charge on national funds, and they recommended that if any Exchequer money was forthcoming at all it should be expended first on the preservation of the sea coast. They noted that a long stretch of coast-line was still unprotected. On the question of controlling development in the countryside the Committee found that, in spite of the fact that if compensation were faced the 1932 Act powers to control inappropriate development were practically unlimited, none of the rural zoning methods then in general use were entirely appropriate to the completely rural area. They proposed instead a new rural zoning under which all development which was not agricultural or rural in character would be subject to close scrutiny.

In December 1938, the Ministry of Health Circular 1750 recommended the Advisory Committee's Report for consideration by Planning Authorities. The Circular put forward the rural zone suggested by the Advisory Committee and also certain variations of it suitable for use on lands immediately adjoining the coast. It was felt that the use of the rural zone would make it largely unnecessary for agreements to be negotiated for the reservation of private open spaces. It was recognised that as a means of dealing with extensive areas planning by way of formal agreement had been troublesome and rather unsatisfactory.[7]

In another sphere, too, the reliance on formal agreements to reserve land was seen to be inadequate. This was the case of the green belt. The idea of a London Green Belt began in 1927 with the Greater London Regional Planning Committee, the Technical Director of which was Dr. Raymond Unwin. Their Interim and Final Reports in 1929 and 1933 advocated a green girdle round London to contain urban spread and to preserve the rapidly diminishing supply of land which was suitable for recreation purposes. For financial reasons little progress was made at first with the actual acquisition, or sterilisation from building, of such land, but for a number of years Middlesex and Surrey C.C.s in particular

---

* The Minister of Health (Hilton Young) and the Secretary of State for Scotland received a deputation on 14 March 1933 from the Amenities Group of Members of the House of Commons; also present were representatives of the National Trust and the C.P.R.E. The Amenities Group had resolved that the Minister and the Secretary of State be urged to set up Advisory Committees on the lines of the Royal Fine Art Commission as suggested in the Report of the National Parks Committee.

were active in acquiring land for regional open spaces. The North Middlesex Green Belt was recommended by the North Middlesex Regional Town Planning Committee and provisionally approved by the Minister.[8] In 1933, with an improved financial situation, the Minister announced that favourable consideration would be given to applications for loan sanction for acquisition of land for open space where it could be shown that only immediate acquisition would save the land from building. Later, the L.C.C. decided to contribute up to 50% of the capital cost of acquiring open spaces in the Greater London area, subject to a maximum for the three years beginning 1935–36 of £2 millions. By the end of March 1939 the L.C.C. had approved areas totalling 70,650 acres and had made provisional offers of assistance for the purchase of land for the green belt amounting to £1,874,000.

But a dual system of entering into formal agreements and grant-aided acquisition was not enough and the L.C.C. promoted a Bill for the preservation of the green belt. The Green Belt (London and Home Counties) Act, 1938, allowed owners of land, local authorities and parish councils to enter into covenants restrictive of users and for local authorities to acquire by agreement; there were also certain statutory powers of acquisition.

National Parks

In September 1929 the Prime Minister (J. Ramsay MacDonald), as a result of representations made to the effect that suitable lands should be reserved for use as National Parks on the lines of those in the U.S.A. and Canada, appointed a Committee of Inquiry to examine the proposal. The terms of reference were 'to consider and report if it is desirable and feasible to establish one or more National Parks in Great Britain with a view to the preservation of natural characteristics including flora and fauna, and to the improvement of recreational facilities for the people; and to advise generally and in particular as to the areas, if any, that are most suitable for the purpose.' The Chairman was Christopher Addison, who became Minister of Agriculture and Fisheries in June 1930.

The Committee took evidence from a large number of bodies: individuals, and representatives of societies, institutions and committees. The National Trust hoped for Government money annually for the purchase and maintenance of National Parks. The British Correlating Committee for the Protection of Nature emphasised the need of measures for the preservation of flora and fauna and features of special geological interest independently of the recreational aspect of National Parks. The Ramblers' Federations (Glasgow, Huddersfield, Liverpool, London, Manchester and Sheffield) advocated the provision of areas large enough to furnish the greater part of a day's walking. The Pedestrians' Associations drew attention to the invasion of downland, commons and forest by motor vehicles. Campers and Youth Hostellers had their own particular claims. The Art Workers Guild and other societies wished to see parks preserved from commercial exploitation. The Council for the Preservation of Rural Wales urged the choice of Snowdonia and the Pembrokeshire coast. The Town Planning Institute envisaged National Parks as a component part of a nation-wide scheme of parks, open spaces and playing fields. The British Waterworks Association warned of the dangers of including gathering grounds in National Parks. The Automobile Association reflected the interests of the motoring public.

The Committee reported in April 1931 (*Report of the National Park Committee*).[9] They recommended a number of measures, 'necessary if the present generation is to escape the charge that in a short-sighted pursuit of its immediate ends it has squandered a noble heritage' (para. 84). The Committee found that National Parks in the North American sense were not practicable in Britain, but there was a need of adequate measures for preserving the countryside. The Committee's recommendations varied as to what financial assistance could be expected over a five year period. On the assumption that annual sums of the order of £100,000 could be made available, the appointment of two Executive Authorities was recommended: one for England and Wales and one for Scotland with powers to select National Reserve areas. On the assumption that annual sums of not less than £10,000 could be made available then grants should be distributed and the establishment of two Advisory Committees considered.

It was recognised that special measures were needed. The case was as follows: 'there are in this country areas of peculiar interest to the Nation as a whole—typical stretches of coastline, mountainous regions, moor and downs, riverbanks and fen. These areas constitute an important national asset and the Nation cannot afford to take any risk that they will be destroyed or subjected to disorderly development. The extent of the areas in question puts any policy of acquisition, whether by the National Trust or by any other body, out of the question; the total acreage of common land is large but only represents a fraction of these areas; it is manifestly impossible for the Forestry Commission to select lands for afforestation on the basis of their amenity value, although, in fact, the lands most suitable for afforestation are usually situated in the most picturesque parts of the country; and ... we do not think that the responsibility for safeguarding areas of exceptional interest to the Nation should be left to the unaided efforts of the Local Authorities' (para. 14).

In essence the Committee found in favour of a system of National

Reserves and Nature Sanctuaries in order to safeguard areas of exceptional natural interest against disorderly development and speculation; to improve the means of access for pedestrians to areas of natural beauty; and to promote measures for the protection of flora and fauna. In order to execute planning schemes on the comprehensive lines that were required, a National Authority was 'of advantage'. The Committee recognised that the task of the National Authorities would not be easy. 'They will be attacked by those who think that any expenditure on the preservation of the natural beauties of the country is unjustifiable; assailed by enthusiasts who wish to press their own fancies or look for action on more heroic lines; importuned by private individuals who see in the proposals an opportunity of private gain; and opposed by others who resent any interference with private interests. In many cases they will be called upon to hold an even balance between conflicting interests, and at all times they must be prepared to take a long view, and to leave it to time and a later generation to vindicate their actions' (para. 84). This was a prediction that might well summarise many of the conflicting views current in the whole of the subsequent debate about National Parks, from the 1940s through to the 1960s.

No Government action was taken on the Addison Report, but a considerable and influential lobby had been encouraged. In 1936 the Councils for the Preservation of Rural England and Rural Wales set up a Standing Committee on National Parks under the chairmanship of Sir Norman Birkett. On the Committee were representatives of the Association for the Preservation of Rural Scotland and representatives of many voluntary organisations including the National Trust and the Commons, Open Spaces and Footpaths Preservation Society. The Standing Committee's policy was essentially that put forward in the Addison Report, but the views were to be expressed more forcefully, with a single-mindedness of purpose, and in a way designed to secure popular support. Their pamphlet, *The Case for National Parks in Great Britain* (July 1938), presented the arguments. Professor G. M. Trevelyan's foreword began: 'The Government is at present engaged on a Health Campaign. It undertakes to assist the health of the nation and to find playing fields for the dwellers in the vast cities to play cricket and football. But it is no less essential, for any national health scheme, to preserve for the nation walking grounds and regions where young and old can enjoy the sight of unspoiled nature. And it is not a question of physical exercise only, it is also a question of spiritual exercise and enjoyment. It is a question of spiritual values. Without vision the people perish and without sight of the beauty of nature the spiritual power of the British people will be atrophied.'

The strength of this lobby was of great importance. Its case was well argued, its support extended widely, and amongst its advocates there were important public figures.

Access to Countryside

Public pressure to secure and maintain adequate access to the countryside was exerted through a number of lobbies and interest groups. For example, the Commons, Open Spaces and Footpaths Preservation Society was an active influence. At the very beginning of our period, in 1938, the Society asked the Minister of Health to call the attention of local authorities to the desirability of including in Schemes provision for new cross-country footpaths, especially ridge walks in hill country and connecting field paths to link existing pedestrian routes.[10] As another instance, a Coastal Preservation Committee was set up by the Society, the National Trust and the C.P.R.E.; its Chairman was Lord Merthyr of the National Trust.

But the most important question of the day can be summarised as 'access to mountains'. It was an issue of long standing, beginning with a campaign by James Bryce against the enclosure of Scottish deer forests; he introduced his Access to Mountains (Scotland) Bill in 1884. There was a number of subsequent attempts at legislation but all proved abortive. Bryce's Bill was first introduced to apply to England and Wales in 1888. Twenty years later (1908) a Bill was introduced similar to Bryce's, but it was applicable to Scotland as well as England and Wales. It sought to give the public a restricted right to walk on certain private property without being subject to the law of trespass. Further Bills followed in 1924, 1926, 1927, 1928, 1930 and 1931.

Geoffrey Mander's Access to Mountains Bill was introduced in October 1937; it was issued in February 1938 and came up for Second Reading later that month. Its object, reflecting the theme of previous attempts, was 'to secure to the public the right of free access to uncultivated mountain and moorland, subject to proper provisions for preventing any abuse of such right'. A Home Office view was that 'the principle of the Bill is one to which most people would subscribe, but the extent of its application is obscure and the provisions for preventing abuse are obviously inadequate'.[11] The Bill was blocked (after it not being reached on a Friday) largely on account of the inadequate provision made for the protection of owners and occupiers, whose only remedy for any abuse would have been an action for trespass.

Earlier Bills had turned largely on the exclusion of a limited public from land reserved for shooting. But the situation was now different. In the 1930s the questions concerned rambling and the use of land by the general public on a much more extensive scale. The problem areas were the grouse moors of the North, where the conflict was between the interests of landowners and of ramblers and other community groups concerned with countryside access. Throughout 215 square miles of moorland area in and adjacent to the Peak District for example, there were only twelve footpaths which exceeded two miles in length, and none of the principal heights of the area were accessible except by trespass. In the West Riding there were vast stretches of moorland with no paths admitted. In the North Riding there were restrictive notices on Goathland Moors. There were other restrictions for different reasons, all of which compounded the public agitation. In the Lake District routes were closed on account of afforestation; in Lancashire the Bowland Forest area had restrictions, and over wide areas the Waterworks Authorities closed considerable tracts. The thirties was a decade when rambling was fashionable; the northern industrial cities spawned their weekend hikers and there was a popular demand for access to moorland areas. But there were additional problems, away from the moorlands. The ramblers found that the Rights of Way Act, 1932, favoured the landowner and placed no compulsion on local authorities to do their duty with regard to footpath provision. There were instances of footpath closure and only one County Council, Essex, had undertaken to signpost its footpaths.

The Bill of 1937, blocked in February 1938, was the last attempt at legislation which failed to reach the Statute Book. It failed largely on account of the inadequate provision then made for the protection of owners and occupiers of land whose only remedy for any abuse would have been an action for trespass. When Mr. Creech Jones (Member for Shipley) introduced his Bill later in 1938 he was careful to extend the abuses and make them offences. It was a short and simple Bill of five sections, but it was to be considerably amended during its course through the House. In essence it was designed to ensure that persons were not to be prevented from walking on mountain or moorland for the purposes of recreation; in any proceedings for trespass it should be sufficient defence that the lands referred to were uncultivated mountain or moorland; that the defendant entered only for the purposes of recreation or of scientific or artistic study, and that no special damage resulted. However, for persons going on to this land for other purposes (such as in pursuit of game) and where certain undesirable actions took place (disturbance to sheep or cattle or deposit of litter for example) then fines not exceeding forty shillings could be imposed. The Bill did not extend to young plantations or to land 'occupied and enjoyed as a park or pleasure ground in connection with and in proximity to a dwelling house'.

At first the Bill was the concern of the Home Office, but it was clear that no Ministry was keen to handle it. Some regarded the Ministry of Agriculture, as successor to the Enclosure Commissioners, as the appropriate authority. On the other hand, the Ministry of Health, with its concern for physical fitness and in view of previous work on National Parks, might have been seen as appropriate, but there was a marked lack of enthusiasm in this quarter.

As introduced, the Bill still afforded no adequate safeguards to landowners, and when it was considered by the Cabinet on 30 November 1938 it was agreed that it should be blocked.[12] At the Second Reading on 2 December 1938 the Under Secretary for the Home Department (Geoffrey Lloyd) indicated a good deal of sympathy but said that 'in our view it is a bad Bill. It is badly drafted, and it suffers from two particular defects. There is no proper definition of land that could be reasonably enforced in an Act of Parliament, and it does not provide any proper redress for the landowner in respect of abuses that may be suffered in admitting people on the land, and that must be properly provided for in any legislation on this subject'. On the other hand, Mr. Creech Jones claimed that he was introducing his Bill at an opportune moment. 'We want a healthy and intelligent people to serve the nation in war and peace', he declared, and referred to the £2 millions physical fitness programme and the creation of new leisure opportunities through holidays with pay.[13]

Mr. Creech Jones introduced his Bill on behalf of English Rambling Associations, and the anticipated opposition at first came from the landowners. But important negotiations had taken place earlier which paved the way for the opposition to be withdrawn. Sir Lawrence Chubb, Secretary of the Commons, Open Spaces and Footpaths Preservation Society had negotiated with the Land Union and the Central Landowners Association with a view to obtaining an acceptable position over the Bill. This was based on a proposal that access to uncultivated lands should be legalised, subject to provisions based on s.193 of the Law of Property Act, 1925. This dealt with the rights of access by the public for air and exercise over land subject to rights of common. It provided that the Minister (of Agriculture) on application, could impose such limitations on, or conditions as to, the exercise of the rights of access as in the Minister's opinion were necessary for preventing any estate, right, or interest of a profitable or beneficial nature in or over or affecting the land from being injuriously affected. The protection of sporting rights was clearly intended. With regard to commons not situated within a borough or urban district the Act afforded no right of access to the public for air and exercise. But the Lord of the Manor or the owner of the soil could voluntarily make a deed declaring that the section of the Act should apply to the land. In this way, from 1 January 1926 (when the 1925 Act came into operation) up to the end of 1937, 99 deeds affecting 111,955 acres, had been made giving the public right of access for air and exercise to commons in rural districts.

During the debate on the Second Reading, discussions between the promoters and opponents of the Bill suggested that a compromise was possible. With the agreement of the Home Secretary and the Chief Whip, the Under Secretary of State left the Bill to a free vote. He mentioned that if the Bill received Second Reading the Committee stage might be deferred to some extent in the hope that the negotiations which had been mentioned might lead to an agreement which could be embodied in the Bill. The idea was generally welcomed and it was on this understanding that the landowners' representatives withdrew their opposition; the Bill was read a second time without a division.

Accordingly, Mr. Creech Jones deferred the Committee Stage pending the result of negotiations between Sir Lawrence Chubb and the landowners' organisations. Sir Lawrence presented the landowners with a revised Bill empowering the Minister of Agriculture to impose additional restrictions upon the exercise of the proposed rights of access (as in the case of commons under s.193 of the Law of Property Act, 1925). Sir Lawrence had sent copies to the Ministry of Agriculture and the Home Office. The former had statutory duties in respect of commons but felt that the regulation of the public on uncultivated land generally to be outside their province. From the Home Office (Mr. L. N. Blake Odgers) came the suggestion that provision should be made for the Act to operate only when some representing authority had submitted proposals as regards specified land, and the responsible department had approved the proposal subject to any restrictions that might be necessary. A meeting was held in the Home Office on 30 January 1939 with Odgers as Chairman, with representatives of Government Departments and Sir Lawrence Chubb to consider the situation.[14]

The Home Office suggestion as to the operation of the Act was found to be acceptable. The meeting agreed generally that right of access should only come into operation after approval of an application relating to particular land with such restrictions as appeared reasonable to the responsible department. Furthermore it was agreed that the body making the representation should bear expenses involved in giving effect to applications, for example advertisement, provision of signposts, and warning notices. It was felt that this procedure would get over the otherwise insuperable difficulty of defining the land to which the Bill applied. From this point onwards the essence of the Bill became fixed, and the implications of the new proposals provided reason for sharp controversy.

Mr. Creech Jones accepted these conclusions and persuaded both the Ramblers' Associations and the two bodies of landowners to agree in principle to a revised Bill. The agreement of the landowners was obtained largely by offering to include in the Bill a provision by which the landowners themselves would be able to obtain the application of the restrictions to specified land by depositing a deed permitting public access. It was believed there were a number of cases in which a landowner would be glad to allow public access for the sake of the penalty provisions attached to the restrictions in these new proposals.

Agreement was reached in February between the promoters of the Bill and representatives of the landowners led by Lord Radnor (Central Landowners Association) as to the basis on which the Bill should proceed. A drafting Committee consisting of the promoters and landowners' legal advisers now engaged in preparing a revised Bill. But this procedure could not be followed because Mr. Creech Jones was advised that if he did not go into Committee at an early date (first of all 2 March 1939, then 7 March) his Bill would have to go to the bottom of the list. He therefore put down amendments. The landowners agreed to these on the basis that the Ministry of Agriculture would be the Department to administer the Bill; the Central Landowners Association would not hear of the Ministry of Health in this capacity. This obligation filled the Ministry of Agriculture with considerable alarm. The future was problematical because they had no idea of the amount of work that would be encountered, but they recognised that it would be unwise to let slip an opportunity of agreement on a contentious problem.

A Cabinet Memorandum[15] by the Minister of Agriculture and the Secretary of State for Home Affairs on 28 February explained that the negotiations had been 'accepted by a great majority of the English Rambling Associations' and were now embodied in amendments which had the effect of a very different and much longer Bill. Only a few words of the original Bill were retained and the scope had been enlarged to extend to the seashore.

The essence of the Bill was now as follows. The responsible Minister was empowered on application (and after holding a public enquiry if necessary) to apply the Bill by Order to specified land— with additional restrictions if necessary. Applications for Orders might come from a landowner, a local authority (including a parish council) or a rambling association. Landowners were empowered voluntarily to secure the application of the Bill to specified land by depositing a deed with the responsible department. Penalties were imposed for a list of offences; the list had been extended considerably from the original Bill. As framed, the Bill applied to Scotland, but it was understood that Scottish ramblers might ask for Scotland to be excluded. In that event, the promoters would agree; and in fact it was later decided that the Bill should not extend to Scotland. In view of the fact that trespass in Scotland was not an actionable wrong as it was in England, it was appreciated that the Scottish ramblers might take the view that they were better off under their law as it stood than they would be under a Bill with a right of access coupled with conditions and penalties.

The two Ministers felt that 'it would be a pity to let the opportunity slip of enabling the general public to have increased rights of air and exercise subject to reasonable restrictions for preventing damage being done to the interests of those who own the land over which the rights are to be granted'. They recommended that the Cabinet should give general approval to the new proposals.

A number of amendments were placed on the Paper on behalf of water undertakers and local authorities who were also water undertakers. They pressed for exempted land to include that belonging to statutory water undertakers. This followed the lines of observations made earlier (in December 1938) from the Secretary of the Association of Municipal Corporations to the Secretary of the Ministry of Health that land acquired by local authorities in the gathering grounds of reservoirs should be excluded from the operation of the Bill. The Committee took the view that water undertakers were entitled to no more protection than a private owner of land. The Bill provided that access was only to be granted to land in respect of which an Order is made by the Minister; if special protection were needed then the water undertakers could appear at an enquiry that was held.

More serious opposition came from another quarter.[16] In April it became clear that the ramblers did not concur with the outcome of the negotiations with the landowners in February and did not support the Bill as it then stood. On 18 April 1939 the Manchester and District Ramblers Federation Executive Committee adopted two resolutions; namely that the form of the Bill did not safeguard the rights of the public as had been hoped for; and that they strongly opposed the trespass clause.

The case was put strongly in a letter from the Sheffield Ramblers, also dated 18 April 1939, with 12 signatories.* They noted that the Bill had been changed 'from one giving general access to all uncultivated mountain and moorland, to one which only provides costly and cumbersome machinery for obtaining limited access to specific areas, and leaves entirely at the discretion of the Minister of Agriculture the scope and nature of the access to be enjoyed by the

---

* Ernest A. Baker, Phil Barnes, Alfred J. Brown, C. E. M. Joad, Stephen E. Morton, Lilian Robinson, Edwin Royce, Alfred M. Sclater, Kenneth Spence, Tom Stephenson, W. S. Tysoe, and G. H. B. Ward.

public. Agreement to this alteration was only secured by a small majority vote at a hastily convened meeting in London at which certain Ramblers' Federations were not represented and there is a strong body of opinion in the North against this fundamental change.' The letter went on to register 'vehement' opposition to a trespass clause which had been introduced during the Committee stage. They made it clear that this was 'not an agreed Bill' as far as they were concerned. This statement put quite a different complexion on the situation as described in the Cabinet Paper of 28 February.

These views were developed when a deputation from the Ramblers Association* was received by the Parliamentary Secretary on 15 May 1939.[17] The Ramblers had wished to see the Law of Property Act, 1925, adopted as a model for the new machinery: that Act gave automatic access over urban common lands and it was for the objectors to make applications. In the present Bill no immediate access was given and access would depend on initiative being taken by one of three bodies concerned—the ramblers, the landowners and the local authorities. The ramblers believed that the other two would be unlikely to apply for Orders and they themselves would have to apply for the Orders, in which case the financial burden of the legal process would be beyond them. Furthermore, there was objection to clauses on offences and enforcement. For example there was the requirement whereby the name and address of persons suspected of trespassing must be given. In particular the Trespass Clause was strongly resented because it had the effect of making a person walking freely on open moorland in certain circumstances into a criminal. Why, the deputation argued, was the ordinary law of trespass, sufficient up to the present, no longer adequate for the future? The deputation expressed the view that they would rather not have any Bill if the penalty clause were to remain. But from the Government side Lord Radnor said that the Bill had been the subject of long negotiations and that any material change now would upset the agreement obtained; the Bill was aimed as much at the ill-disposed landlord as at the misbehaved ramblers.

The matter of the Trespass Clause originated with the draft Bill submitted in January 1939 by Sir Lawrence Chubb to representatives of the Ramblers Federation. The clause in this draft provided that land controlled under the Act might be closed to the public for specified periods, and that any person found on the land at such a time would be liable to a fine of £2. The clause was designed to meet the landowners' opposition who wanted to close moors and mountains during the lambing weeks, grouse nesting, and the grouse-

---

* A. J. Brown, Phil Barnes, G. H. Ward and C. E. M. Joad.

shooting and deer-stalking seasons. The ramblers strongly objected to this clause on the grounds that it meant a serious alteration of the common law of trespass, and that a grouse moor could thereby be more stringently controlled than a good agricultural land. The clause was deleted from the Draft. But when the Bill emerged from Standing Committee it was found that the Trespass Clause had been reinserted.

Towards the end of the deputation Mr. Fred Marshall, M.P., who had introduced the Ramblers, suggested that a clause be inserted in the Bill suspending the operation of the Trespass Clause for a period of five years, with a view to revision in the light of the experience gained. This was taken up some days later when, on 23 May 1939, Mr. Alex McIntosh, Chairman of the Ramblers Association, wrote to Lord Feversham at the Ministry of Agriculture.[18] He reminded him of the intense feeling among law-abiding ramblers against the Clause which they felt placed them in the position of becoming criminals and in a position of inferiority to the poacher. He wrote, 'I have had no opportunity for consulting my association, but several leading members and I are very strongly of the opinion that if a suspensory clause could be made operative for a period of years it would make a difference of first class importance. I firmly believe that if this were done there would be an excellent chance of the Ramblers' Association working the Bill in good spirit.' He urged an amendment on these lines.

Lord Feversham got the promoters of the Bill to propose an amendment which he sent Mr. Marshall on 24 May. The effect of the amendment was that, unless it was essential in the public interest, the Minister's original order under Clause 3 of the Bill would not make it an offence to enter on to land from which the public were excluded either permanently or temporarily, but that he would have the power to make an amending order, making it an offence so to do, if it were known to him that it was necessary to do so to prevent the continuance of contraventions or of failure to observe conditions or limitations imposed in an order. This was acceptable to Mr. Marshall, and he replied to the effect that he thought the suggested modifications would make the Bill more acceptable to the Rambling Associations.

There were other attempts, successful as well as unsuccessful to weaken the penalty clauses of the Bill. Under Clause 7, £2 fines could be imposed for breach of the conditions laid down in the Act or in an Order made thereunder, provided that a person shall not be guilty of an offence by reason only of any unintentional trespass. Both in Committee and on Report it was argued that the word 'unintentional' should be omitted, but amendments to this effect were defeated. However, in Committee of the House of Lords a proviso was successfully inserted to the effect that failure to observe a condition of an Order should be punishable by fine only if the Order expressly so provided, and that the Minister should not so provide unless satisfied that it is necessary so to do in order to prevent the continuance of contraventions of the condition or in the public interest.[19]

It was in this climate of last ditch compromises and opposition by the ramblers that the Bill went through the House. Mr. H. W. Pegler, Secretary of the Camping Club of Great Britain and Ireland wrote to the Minister of Agriculture on 19 May to say that they associated themselves with the resolution of the Ramblers Association to the effect that it found the Access to Mountains Bill entirely unacceptable. A letter from the Brighton Rambling Club on 17 June to Major Tryon, M.P., expressed the view that it was 'far better to postpone the whole thing'. The Manchester and District Ramblers Federation held their annual joint demonstration in the Winnats Pass in the Peak on 25 June and agreed to a resolution which 'strongly disapproves of those provisions of the Access to Mountains Bill whereby the financial liability of obtaining access is made a burden on ramblers, and of the trespass penalty fine'.[20]

But the time had come for final decisions, although by now the arguments for and against the Bill had become finely balanced. The points in favour were primarily threefold. First, the original Bill only applied to mountains and moors. The scope was now enlarged to embrace heaths, downs and cliffs. Second, public access to such land was gained once the Minister made an Order. Third, viewed pragmatically, the cumbrous machinery which the Act implied was inevitable, if the support and goodwill of the landed interests were to be gained. For example, incursion into the law of trespass might be objected to as a restrictive evil, but could be regarded as the price of the Bill.

Contrary views were expressed as follows. In the first place, the Bill was in sharp contrast to the cardinal principle that people had a right to wander freely over mountain and moorland. Moreover, the Bill itself gave no access anywhere, merely machinery for obtaining it. Much depended on the operation of the Act and the record of Ministers in granting Orders, before one could tell whether the legislation was going to be effective or not. Further, it was argued that the Bill made a piecemeal approach, and innumerable applications would be required to secure right of access to the un-cultivated lands of England and Wales. Another argument was that the cost of putting the legislation into effect would fall largely on the ramblers. It was true that local authorities of more than 20,000 population could also act, but many of these were themselves the owners of sporting moors which they kept closed to the public.

Finally, it was considered that ramblers were in a less advantageous position than they had been before, for a number of statutory offences were created when certain misdeeds were committed on the land. The Act varied the common law of trespass by making it, under some circumstances, a criminal offence to be on access land.

There was a sufficient measure of agreement in Parliament; the Bill went through and secured the Royal Assent on 13 July 1939. The Act came into operation on 1 January 1940. Draft Regulations for the Act, prescribing the procedure to be followed in connection with the making of applications for Orders under the Act were made after consultations with Mr. Creech Jones and Sir Lawrence Chubb. They were advertised in the *London Gazette* in March, the 40 days allowed for receipt of representations expiring on 8 May 1940. The only criticism of substance came from the Sheffield Ramblers *via* Fred Marshall. They felt that the Rules and Orders were more onerous and costly than they had expected.[21] For example there was an unexpected requirement that an Applicant who applied for and obtained an Access Order on behalf of the public was compelled to purchase, erect and maintain for ever elaborately worded Notice Boards.

The Minister's Legal Advisers recommended that no changes in the draft were called for, and the Statutory Rules and Orders were published on 15 May 1940.* It was subsequently decided that during 'the present emergency' no applications for Orders would be dealt with unless they were agreed by all parties. In the event, no application for Orders was ever received. The legislation was completely abortive, suffering the fate of an unsuccessful compromise measure.

But the issues behind the question of access to the countryside were not dead. Indeed they were to reappear in a different and more comprehensive context, that of National Parks. Problems relating to footpaths, rights of way and rambling access were looked at again in the early war years, and it is to this period we should now turn. We may regard the Access to Mountains Act, 1939, as the utmost that the landed and sporting interests were prepared to concede at that time. The next few years eroded that position considerably.

---

* No. 746, *Access to Mountains, England and Wales.*

CHAPTER 3

Advocates for Action

WITHIN the context of wide-ranging ideas concerning the planned reconstruction of Britain after the war, renewed proposals for National Parks and countryside areas took on a new significance. A number of bodies were quick to publish their views. The Commons, Open Spaces and Footpaths Preservation Society produced a 13-page note, *Memorandum on Post War Planning* in September 1941; this dealt with the preservation of open spaces, rights of public access, and the question of National Parks. It was duly referred to the Amenities Sub-committee of the Advisory Committee on Reconstruction of the Office of Works. The Society for the Promotion of Nature Reserves issued a Conference Memorandum, *Nature Preservation in Post War Reconstruction*, in November 1941. At about the same time the Ramblers Association issued *Proposed Post War Country and Town Planning: with particular reference to Access, National Parks and Footpaths*.

Of all such pressure groups, the continual lobby of the Standing Committee on National Parks of the Councils for the Preservation of Rural England and Wales was most marked. Under the Chairmanship of Norman Birkett, K.C., the Standing Committee of the two Councils had worked since 1936 to gather support for the provision of National Parks. Its composition embraced a wide cross section of countryside and recreation opinion. The two Councils were represented by their presidents, chairmen, honorary treasurers and secretaries. Other members represented the following: Royal Automobile Club, Automobile Association, Geographical Association, National Trust, Camping Club, Fell and Rock Climbing Club, Commons, Open Spaces and Footpaths Preservation Society, Royal Society for the Protection of Birds, Holiday Fellowship, Society for the Promotion of Nature Reserves and Wild Plant Conservation Board, Ramblers Association, Alpine Club, Youth Hostels Association, Cyclists Touring Club, Co-operative Holiday Association, Pedestrians Association, the Zoological Society and the Society for Protection of the Fauna of the Empire. There were co-opted members and there was a representative of the Association for the Preservation of Rural Scotland. This was a formidable array of associated interests.

27

The general objectives of the Standing Committee were two-fold: first, that a sufficient number of extensive areas, carefully selected from the unspoilt wilder country of Great Britain, should be strictly preserved and specifically run as National Parks; and second, that the remainder of the unspoilt wilder country should be regarded as a reserve for further National Parks in the future. These objectives were based essentially on policies put forward in the Addison Report on National Parks, 1931.

By 1939 the Standing Committee had already prepared a summary of the required provisions for a Bill to establish National Parks. These were not then presented to Government because of the unsuitable timing, but in November 1941 Birkett offered the summary to Lord Reith at the Ministry of Works and Buildings for his consideration. He commended the note in an accompanying letter: 'I think you will be very willing to give them weight in your preparations for post-war planning.'[22] The note recommended the setting up of a National Parks Commission, and the provision of Government funds to cover its administrative expenses, plus a lump sum of £500,000 for use in acquisition of land, grants and compensations. It went on to outline a comprehensive scheme. The Commission, advised by a National Parks Consultative Council, would designate National Parks, National Park Access Areas and National Nature Sanctuaries. For each National Park the Commission would set up an Advisory Committee of local representatives. The Commission would be the planning authority for every National Park; it would prepare planning schemes and have power of control over all development of land. The Commission would prepare and publish lists and maps of all footpaths and bridleways and would have power to create and pay for new ones. The general public would have access to all parts of any National Park Access Area as if it were a common, subject to s.193 of the Law of Property Act, 1925. The Commission would make regulations for the strict preservation of flora and fauna and of rocks of geological interest in National Nature Sanctuaries. The Commission would appoint Preservation Wardens.

Birkett asked Reith for an informal meeting with members of the Standing Committee, and this was arranged for 6 January 1942.* Those attending with Birkett were Professor Patrick Abercrombie (Chairman C.P.R.E.; Professor of Town Planning, University of London), Rev. H. H. Symonds (Youth Hostels Association, London Secretary of the Standing Committee), the Earl of Onslow (President of the Society for Preservation of Nature Reserves and of the Society

---

* We should take care to note that this was not the only approach on this subject to Reith at this time. A deputation from the National Trust was received by him in December 1941. Additionally, the President of the Society for the Promotion of Nature Reserves (Lord Macmillan) on several occasions asked the Minister to come and speak to them.

for Empire Fauna Protection), W. L. Platts (Vice Chairman of the County Councils Association; Clerk, Kent C.C.) and G. F. Herbert Smith (London Secretary of the Society for the Preservation of Nature Reserves).

At the meeting Birkett repeated the Standing Committee's general approach, namely that the Addison Report (and the Ministry of Health subsequently) had assumed that National Parks could largely be secured by means of Planning Schemes, facilitated in particular by the Town and Country Planning Act, 1932. This assumption could no longer be held. Small, rural, local authorities possessed neither the means nor the incentive to take the initiative; nor were they powerful enough to stand up to statutory undertakers, Government Departments or to industrial interests. Limestone blasting and cement manufacture in the Peak District and war factories in the Lake District were given as instances of what was happening. Abercrombie added to the story of failure by referring to the position of joint planning. In the Lake District the counties had not co-operated to secure either the definition of a National Park area or one Joint Committee for the whole. Planning schemes had been prepared for parts, but fears of compensation had made them weak. One scheme was instanced which proposed to leave administration to an impecunious Rural District Council whose officer for the purpose would be the Sanitary Inspector.

Lord Onslow stressed the need for the protection of fauna. He wanted reservations for animals in large areas, national in character and provided for out of rates. Abercrombie included this aim in a three-fold objective: continuation of agricultural use, natural recreation for the public, and preservation of flora and fauna. Reith declared himself in favour of these three points. Perhaps he had in mind that he had appointed a Committee only three months earlier (October 1941) under the chairmanship of Lord Justice Scott to consider a number of matters very similar to Abercrombie's. But he went on to ask questions. For example, what constituted a National Park area? Should these areas be purchased by the local authorities responsible? Would the National Trust be a suitable holding authority?

There could be no immediate answer. Many issues were involved, and it was agreed that Vincent and Pepler from Reith's Ministry should meet informally with Abercrombie, Platts and Symonds to consider further details. There is no record of a meeting of such a continuation committee,* but John Dower, also of the Minister's staff, helped Symonds and the Standing Committee to draw up a possible list of National Park areas. This schedule, subsequently

---

* A memo from G. S. Pepler to the Minister of Town and Country Planning on 20 August 1943 states 'I do not think we ever met as a group'. (File 95249/19)

sent to Lord Portal when Minister of Works and Planning, suggested that Northern England, Southern England and Wales should have an equal number of Parks. Six were proposed as a minimum first selection: Lake District, Dartmoor, Snowdonia, Peak District, South Downs and Pembroke Coast. A further nine were proposed for later consideration, keeping the geographical balance: Craven Pennines, North Cornish Coast and Black Mountains; Roman Wall, Exmoor and Brecon Beacons; Cheviots, White Horse Hills and Plynlimmon.

The Standing Committee continued to apply pressure in other Government circles. An important meeting was held on 8 April 1942 when a delegation from the Standing Conference met the Paymaster General, Sir William Jowitt. The delegates comprised Mr. Trustram Eve, Sir Norman Birkett (Chairman), Professor Abercrombie, Professor Chorley, and Rev. H. H. Symonds, the Committee's drafting secretary. Birkett introduced the discussion by referring to the past struggle of many voluntary Societies against defacement of the countryside; the demands of the Service Departments now made their task more difficult. Abercrombie described the dangers against which the powers of planning authorities were quite inadequate. He cited the activities of Government Departments, statutory undertakers, local authorities (particularly in reservoir construction), mineral workers, the tourist industry and private house builders in beauty spots. Above all, there was the inability of local authorities to pay necessary compensation. There was sufficient in the delegation's points of view for the matter to be kept alive, and the Paymaster General asked the Committee to furnish him with a letter setting out their plans and estimating their cost, which he would then submit to the Chancellor.[23]

Another delegation shortly afterwards, this time from the Conference on Nature Preservation in Post War Reconstruction,* also met Sir William Jowitt, on 4 May 1942.[24] The Conference had been interested in the maintenance of three types of area. First, there were large open spaces primarily intended for public recreation, such as Snowdonia, the Lakes and the Peak district. Second, there were other large areas selected for purposes of nature reservation where the survival of certain threatened species could be assured. Third, there were small areas where rare or local species flourished and could easily be protected. The spokesman for the delegates, Mr. W. L. Platts (Lord Onslow not being able to attend), urged that these areas be identified so that they could be fitted in to post-war planning

---

* The Society for the Promotion of Nature Reserves called a Conference at the House of Lords in June 1941 under the chairmanship of Lord Onslow to discuss a proposed memorandum to the Prime Minister and Lord Reith on the question of Nature Reserves and National Parks. The Standing Committee were not in agreement with this memorandum, but the Conference was set up for the following year.

schemes. Another delegate, Captain Diver, advised that a scientific body be appointed to draw up detailed proposals for the establishment of reserves, and the Minister expressed sympathy with this suggestion. Furthermore, the Minister thought that a Committee would be useful to represent their point of view, and the delegates undertook to suggest suitable terms of reference and membership.

Sir William Jowitt in a note to Lord Portal thought that these two deputations made 'a good case for the establishment of Reserves, both from the point of view of preserving for posterity unspoiled samples of the countryside with their characteristic wild life and the far more important cause of providing the means for public outdoor recreation'.[25] But there was resistance to the idea of an independent National Park Authority, as advocated by the Addison Report of 1931, and which was strongly supported by the Standing Committee on National Parks. The Chancellor of the Exchequer, Kingsley Wood, thought it a mistake to create a new Authority with specific powers in respect of a particular kind of land and new vested interests when planning on a new and wide scale with regard to land utilisation in general was being considered. There was also the question of providing substantial funds for such a new Authority, as there would be many other post-war priorities. The conclusion was that it was not the time to establish an independent Authority and that it was preferable to build on existing agencies and powers. National Parks could not take a very high place in the queue for national funds.[26] At Kingsley Wood's suggestion, however, a small, informal group, on which the Treasury was represented, was set up to consider possible future action; the chairman was J. M. Tucker, K.C. But it was soon decided that no further action should be taken until after the Scott and Uthwatt Reports had been received.

In the meantime, the Standing Committee continued to marshal its energies effectively and became a persistent and cogent advocate for National Parks. At the end of April Lord Portal was another Minister (Works and Planning) to receive a copy of its argument 'Why a National Park Commission and not merely a strengthening of the planning authorities?'[27] In some ways this was a repetition of the case outlined in the Summary which Lord Reith had received, but the argument was now becoming more forceful. The opening paragraph outlined a general scheme. 'To establish National Parks some executive power is needed which is persistent and settled in its aim and method, specialised in its application, and independent of political change and pressure. Clearly National Parks must be one part of the master-plan for land utilisation: none the less the policy which is to create and maintain them is a distinguishable part of this plan, aiming at a more determinate and relatively final purpose. The Ministry of Planning, which deals with a subject matter that must always change and develop as science and industry and international trade change and develop, will be distracted by the width and complexity of its duties: for National Parks, what is needed is a body specially appointed and directed by Act of Parliament, a Commission which in the public judgment will stand for a definite and chartered policy. To frame and to execute such a policy, a special and whole-time personnel is needed, chosen for its skill and enthusiasm. By the terms of its appointment it must be protected from confusion and multiplicity of aims and be concentrated on a specific task; and it must be protected from any weakening of its purpose or any lapse of power, through political change. It is to be remembered that National Parks are, in the best sense, a popular cause, with a place in the public imagination: a formed public opinion supports and demands them. On the other hand, Town and Country Planning, as such, is too technical a cause—and also too wide—ever to be "popular". But a separation of National Parks from the general administration of Town and Country Planning, and the creation of a single and manageable instrument to disentangle them out of surrounding complexities, will give to a specific demand a specific and intelligible answer. A Commission will have the momentum to succeed. The Commissioners will have the momentum to succeed. The Commissioners will hold office for a guaranteed period and cabinet changes will not vary the essential policy and power defined for them by the constitutive Act.'

In that last sentence the case, finally, is almost over-stated: the certainty of being right for all time poses particular questions for any Government. But the articulate quality of the argument, supported by a wide popularity, fuelled the National Parks idea during these formative years. While ever the form and style of post-war planning remained undetermined, the argument for such an *ad hoc* land-use planning body was a strong one. Furthermore, the propagandist drive was particularly forceful at a time of post-war reconstruction when social idealism and unity of purpose was so strongly in evidence. Moreover there was the added advantage of speaking with a single voice. Occasionally, there were examples of some of the constituents of the Standing Committee approaching the Ministry separately, but in the main, there was a unified representation of view. Another feature was that the Standing Committee were constantly alive to significant political opportunities. For example, when W. S. Morrison was appointed Minister of Town and Country Planning, a deputation was soon arranged (on 14 September 1943) from Sir Norman Birkett, Colonel Buxton (National Trust) and Rev. H. H. Symonds. But above all, there was an expressed single-mindedness of purpose about the nature of the administration that was deemed necessary for National Parks. The concluding paragraph of the Report (quoted above) was that 'the creation and administration of National Parks is a special task with its own problems; and therefore requires a specialised and permanent body with powers, defined by the constitutive Act, adequate to achieve the purpose. National Parks will require a special fund, kept in a special account and specially presented to Parliament: responsibility for the right and proper use of this fund should rest upon a special body.' The National Parks debate therefore soon became much more than a matter of principles; the real arguments concerned administrative machinery.

The National Parks lobby had more than a central organ; considerable pressure could be exercised at the regional level and in respect of one particular National Park. This was especially so with the Lake District where there was a singular combination of a number of advantageous factors. The activities of the Friends of the Lake District are illustrative of the agitation during the early and middle 1940s. First, personalities; the President at this time was Sir Norman Birkett, the Vice President initially was the Archbishop of Canterbury and subsequently Archbishop of York, and the secretary was Rev. H. H. Symonds (like the President, of the National Standing Committee). There was no absence of issues, and the way these were seized upon by the Friends are good examples of the running battle between the amenity conscious of the National Parks movement and the many interests of various Government Departments. It is difficult to be certain just when or how far the pressure of the many propagandists tilted the balance in Officials' or Ministers' minds as to the course of future legislation, but it is certain that this formed a most important backcloth against which decisions were made.

The Scott Report

The idea of the Scott Committee originated with Lord Reith. As Minister of Works and Buildings, he was entrusted with responsibility for the guidance and supervision of the preparatory work of formulating the methods and machinery required for the physical reconstruction of town and country after the war. With this brief, Reith began a number of investigations; a study of rural industries was included to obtain information on what industries were suitable for location in country areas. In consultation with the Minister of Agriculture (R. S. Hudson), he appointed a Committee in October 1941 with Lord Justice Scott as chairman. The terms of reference were as follows: 'To consider the conditions which should govern building and other constructional development in country areas consistently with the maintenance of agriculture, and in particular the factors affecting the location of industry, having regard to economic operation, part-time and seasonal employment, the

33

well-being of rural communities and the preservation of rural amenities.' The terms of reference applied to England and Wales and did not include Scotland; as we shall see later, Scotland was the subject of another enquiry (see page 69).

Ministerial confusion at the appointment of this Committee indicated lack of clarity as to where responsibility for planning was then placed. Arthur Greenwood, Minister without Portfolio, complained to Lord Reith that he had not agreed to the terms of reference of the Committee and that there was no consultation with Ernest Brown, Minister of Health (who also complained); moreover, he had difficulty in understanding the exact meaning of the committee's terms of reference.[28] Reith's reply to Greenwood was that consultation had been at Departmental level and maintained that there was no difficulty about terms of reference or poaching on other preserves.[29]

At the request of the Chairman, and confirmed by Lord Reith, the Office of Vice Chairman of the Committee was undertaken by Dr. L. Dudley Stamp, an influential geographer through his earlier work on the Land Utilisation Survey. The Secretary was Thomas Sharp, a town planner with an established interest in this field, as reflected by his publications, *Town and Countryside* (1932) and *English Panorama* (1936). The Committee conducted its work speedily. Written and oral evidence was taken from Government Departments and from many organisations and individual witnesses. The Committee reported in August 1942.[30] Enabled by wide terms of reference, the Committee ranged broadly, and the Scott Report did not have the focus on rural industry that its origins might have implied. The Committee examined the characteristics of the countryside and the nature of recent changes; they reviewed the impact of town on country and the effects of urban growth; they speculated on future trends and considered the adequacy of current planning legislation. A number of recommendations followed in respect of rural conservation, countryside recreation and National Parks.

With regard to the preservation of the countryside, the Scott Report had an important starting point: the Committee regarded 'the countryside as the heritage of the whole nation, and furthermore, we consider that the citizens of this country are the custodians of a heritage they share with all those of British descent and that it is a duty incumbent upon the nation to take proper care of that which it thus holds in trust'. In exercising this duty the Committee considered 'that the land of Britain should be both useful and beautiful and that the two aims are in no sense incompatible'. 'The countryside cannot be "preserved" . . .; it must be farmed if it is to retain these features which give it distinctive charm and character.' Or, in other words, 'even were there no economic, social or strategic reasons for the maintenance of agriculture, the cheapest way, indeed the only way, of preserving the countryside in anything like its traditional aspect would still be to farm it' (para. 160). In the halting progress made towards countryside planning in which National Parks were to have their place, these were fundamental statements.

The planning strategy put forward for rural areas was an inter-related package. There were recommendations for the improvement of rural housing, the provision of electricity, gas and water, and the refocus of cultural life through community or social centres; the provision of new industry in small towns and the encouragement of rural trades and crafts in villages; and the location of building development on less productive land in the light of agriculture. More specifically, there were a number of key statements from the point of view of recreation and the preservation of amenity.

First, in arguing the principle that the countryside was the heritage of all, the Committee accepted the corollary that there should be facility of access for all. The Report recommended that the Board of Education and the Ministry of Agriculture be asked 'to organise a publicity campaign with the bodies concerned to educate the urban public, landowners and farmers with a view to promoting mutual understanding and the better provision of access generally to the countryside' (para. 175). Organised visits of school parties into the country were urged.

Second, the work of the Commons and Footpaths Preservation Society was commended, but the Scott Committee considered that it should be a statutory obligation upon the local planning authority to record on maps and to signpost clearly all undisputed rights of way and to try to resolve all disputed cases. A Footpaths Commission was recommended to investigate disputed cases and give decisions and to recommend the opening of new public footpaths and the closing of old ones. Main 'hikers highways' should be recognised, and the old 'coastguards path' reopened as a right of way round the whole coastline of England and Wales where appropriate.

Third, the Committee thought the establishment of National Parks in Britain to be 'long overdue' (para. 178). They recommended the delimitation of National Parks and the setting up of a national body to control them. As part of this scheme the coast of England and Wales should be considered as a whole with a view to preventing further spoliation. Details of common lands should be recorded to safeguard any public rights of access or use and otherwise to ascertain the position of commoners' rights. The Committee recommended the establishment of Nature Reserves, though separate from National Parks. With regard to recreation in National Parks, the Committee noted the provisions of the Camps Act, 1939, for the facilitation of

35

the construction, maintenance and management of camps of a permanent character. They viewed 'with favour the increase of Youth Hostels, the further provision of camping grounds and camp sites, commercial holiday camps and holiday villages', and it was presumed that appropriate camps would be provided in National Parks.

Fourth, in the consideration of post-war town reconstruction, it was recognised that a lowering of residential densities and over-spill of population would result in the inevitable expansion of the urban area into the countryside. The Committee saw it as the function of the planning authority to determine when a town had reached its maximum or optimum size and when it should be limited by a zone of open land—the green belt. A footnote to para. 202 of the Report clearly defined what was envisaged: 'We conceive the green belt to be a tract of ordinary country, of varying width, round a town, and as a tract where the normal occupations of farming or forestry should be continued so that here, as elsewhere in rural land, the farmer is the normal custodian of the land ... The townsman himself is vitally concerned in the maintenance of the open character of the land and the belt will naturally include golf courses and open common land primarily for his use. On the other hand the farmer is compelled to recognise that the farm land is serving a dual purpose, and that there may be types of farming (e.g. sheep rearing) unsuitable for such an area, where sheer pro-pinquity brings urban minded people into rural surroundings.' In this History we do not examine the contribution of green belt policy to countryside recreation planning, but we should note at this point the comprehensive range of the Scott Report. It was unusual to see the question of footpaths, National Parks and green belts raised in one document.

At its meeting on 18 August 1942, the Reconstruction Problems Committee directed that the Scott Report (and the Uthwatt Report) be referred to the Official Committee on Post War Internal Economic Problems to report 'what recommendations, if any, it would be desirable to adopt, what legislation would be necessitated thereby, and what relationship that legislation would have to the legislation now in course of preparation'. The Chairman, A. W. Hurst, drew up a Memorandum, dated 27 August 1943, which brought together various Departments' views on the Scott recommendations, and which described the measures already in hand on certain of them.* It was in fact an 'interim report setting out the general scope and character of the various recommendations, the action, departmental or otherwise, that is proceeding in the many spheres of Government

---

* See Volume I of this Official History series, *Environmental Planning 1939–69,* J. B. Cullingworth, H.M.S.O., 1975.

administration to which they relate and the extent in each case to which it may now be possible to indicate future Government policy. If thought desirable, this might perhaps form the basis of a Government statement in Parliament on the Scott Report that would put its multifarious collection of recommendations in their proper setting in regard to the various branches of reconstruction policy'.[31]

The report was considered by the War Cabinet Committee on Reconstruction Problems on 9 September 1943 and again a month later on 26 October when Lord Jowitt, Minister without Portfolio, agreed to deal with the Scott Committee's Report by written answer to a question, and not as a White Paper. On 29 October the War Cabinet approved a draft statement[32] on the Report of the Scott Committee. This statement was given by the Minister of Town and Country Planning (W. S. Morrison) in reply to a question in the House on 30 November. He said that the recommendations relating to the preservation of rural amenities and the provision of improved access to the countryside 'are accepted by the Government: the various detailed proposals are under close review by the several Departments concerned with a view to appropriate action. Surveys are being made of areas suitable for national parks, nature reserves and recreational purposes, and a detailed coastal survey is being prepared as a basis for improved measures of access and control. There can be no doubt that the post-war period will see a greatly increased demand for holiday facilities, especially in the country; and the means of providing such facilities, including, in suitable places, the provision of holiday camps, are being worked out by the Departments concerned. In general, the Government accept the view that the natural beauty of our countryside is a matter of national importance and, as such, must be of direct concern to national planning.'

We shall see later how during the early and middle 1940s various statements gave the Government's view on National Parks and countryside affairs with increasing affirmation and intention; one by one they placed the Government in a position of no return on future legislation. The Scott Report played its part in this process. Meanwhile, in Scotland a similar enquiry had been made, followed by encouraging Government comment; this part of the History is given separately (see page 69).

The Dower Report

During August and September 1942 John Dower surveyed possible National Park areas for the Ministry of Works and Planning.[33] These included the Lake District, Snowdonia, the Peak, Pembrokeshire and Dartmoor-Exmoor. His reports for the Department, programmed for the autumn of that year and the spring of 1943,

37

described the characteristics of the areas, their boundaries, problems and requirements. Over the next two years, although interrupted by bouts of ill-health, he laid many important foundations for a subsequent National Parks programme.

Dower's field work contributed to the thinking of the Department on planning matters generally, where Vincent, Holford and Pepler were busy preparing the groundwork for the development of the new planning machine. For example, we read from a letter from Dower to Vincent[34] how he hoped that his boundaries for the Lake District might be regarded as delineating a 'unit planning area' that the Department had in mind for post-war planning units.* His work built up into a comprehensive study and ultimately was published in May 1945; political sensitivity at the time made it a personal Report to the Minister of Town and Country Planning, for information and as a basis for discussion,[35] rather than a Ministerial pronouncement. None the less, it was a timely publication because during the previous three years, since the Scott Report, there had been continued pressure from the lobbies, replied to by cautious but increasingly positive Government statements. There was also pressure as a result of certain developments at local authority level, within the National Park areas. But while National Parks in principle could easily be accepted politically, the necessary machinery of Government was not yet in being to implement them and there was great need for rigorous and practical thinking about the implications involved. The history of National Parks during these years is intimately bound up with the steps taken to set up the new planning machinery for post-war Britain. Caution on the latter implied delay on the former.

The Standing Committee on National Parks kept up the pressure with another broadsheet in December 1944, *National Parks: their creation and administration*. From Government circles various spokesmen alluded to future National Parks and the importance of countryside recreation. In 1944 the White Paper *The Control of Land Use*[36] referred to the preservation of land for National Parks and forests, and 'the assurance to the people of the enjoyment of the sea and countryside in times of leisure' as one part of a single reconstruction programme (para. 1). Later, quite specifically it referred to the establishment of National Parks in national policies (para. 36).

Local authorities had their own view of National Parks and

---

* See J. B. Cullingworth, Vol. I of this Official History series. The War Cabinet had set up an Interdepartmental Committee on Reconstruction under the chairmanship of H. G. Vincent. A sub-committee, chaired by T. D. Harrison, prepared a number of Reports which in fact formed the basis of much of the legislation eventually enacted in the immediate post-war years. In one of these Reports a system of permanent joint planning authorities for the whole of England and Wales was suggested, all of substantial extent in acreage and population to carry an adequate technical staff. There were to be about 200–350 of these unit areas and Dower saw that the Lake District could be one of these.

Government soon found a sensitive problem, which was not easily resolved: the question of the future administration of National Parks in fact became increasingly delicate. The Lake District as a case study offers an example of the difficulties. The Lake District Three Counties Advisory Committee had been established in 1935 to consider the protection of the Lake District under planning schemes. As a result, in Cumberland all the authorities except Keswick U.D.C., Penrith U.D.C. and R.D.C. relinquished their powers to the County Council which worked through Advisory Joint Committees. Keswick insisted on administering its own planning affairs and the two Penrith Councils set up a Penrith and District Joint Committee, which prepared a scheme. In Westmorland, a scheme prepared by the Lake District Joint Planning Committee for the areas of the Lakes U.D. and South Westmorland R.D. became operative on 30 July 1939. Windermere U.D.C. prepared a draft scheme; Kendal passed a resolution to prepare a scheme, and North Westmorland R.D.C. did likewise with reference to their authority near Ullswater. In April 1944 the Westmorland Joint Planning Committee was constituted, of which all the local authorities in the County were constituent members. In Lancashire, the North Lonsdale Joint Committee had been set up. A scheme for Grange U.D. was now in operation and other schemes had been submitted. There was, therefore, some progress towards joint planning, although clearly there were limitations of building up an overall plan from such a base in view of the parochialism of the schemes that had been prepared.

In October 1944 the Clerk of Westmorland informed the Secretary of the Ministry of Town and Country Planning that at a recent conference representatives from the three counties had met to consider the various proposals that had been put forward in different quarters for the establishment of National Parks.[37] By April 1945 the Clerk could write to say that recommendation was being made to all the local authorities to concur in the establishment of a Joint Planning Committee for the area which would fall within the confines of a National Park and to delegate to that Committee their powers of preparing a scheme or revising an existing scheme. In May 1946 the Clerk informed the Secretary that this Joint Planning Committee had been set up. But what might be seen in one quarter as far-sighted and responsive to needs might be seen in another as simply defensive; in a letter to P. T. Mansfield at the Ministry* Dower commented that 'the main and avowed purpose of the Joint Committee is unquestionably local authority self defence against the anticipated central authority "poaching", which is their

---

* 29 June 1946.

version of the future National Park regime'. This episode highlights the different assumptions made about National Park administration by Central and Local Government. For the next few years Government was torn between the advice of those bodies who argued that National Parks were best administered from the centre, and those who argued for local control.

In order that the background to the National Parks story is adequately portrayed, the illustration from the Lake District might be continued; this shows how local sensitivities had to be so carefully handled at this time. In October 1944 the Friends of the Lake District submitted a memorandum to the Minister in which they questioned the adequacy of existing administration for National Parks. They recognised the new provisions of the Town and Country Planning Act, 1943, for creating Joint Committees but stressed that such an arrangement could not be effective for large areas without a National Parks Commission to exercise initiative and to carry final responsibility. The Friends, as self-appointed guardians of amenity, saw overriding merit in a Central Commission with executive powers, which is perhaps why the local authorities reacted defensively and were at pains to sponsor their own Committees; as Dower wrote to Mansfield, 'not entirely without justification, particularly in the Lake District where Symonds' widely publicised claims for an overriding Commission run so high and have provoked so much controversy'.

The administrative and legislative problems involved in the policy of National Parks were highlighted in the Distribution of Industry Bill, 1945, and the Friends were quick to illustrate how the Lake District might be at risk. Within Cumberland there was a long standing division, based on Abercrombie and Kelly's *Cumbrian Regional Report*, 1932, between the Lakeland Planning scheme (non-industrial) and the Northern Planning scheme (industrial West Cumberland). However, the Distribution of Industry Bill scheduled the whole area of the Lakeland Planning Scheme as part of the West Cumberland Development Area. The Friends therefore obtained the official support of the Standing Committee on National Parks and of the National Trust, and arranged for an amendment to the schedule in the Bill. The general effect of this was to exclude from the proposed Development Area all the territory within the Lakeland Planning Scheme except near the Royal Ordnance Factory at Sellafield and around Millom.

Hugh Dalton, President of the Board of Trade, accepted the main principle of this amendment, though he reserved for inclusion in the Development Area the Cumberland coast-line. Just before the Whitsun recess he tabled an official amendment, which as a Government proposal would have been carried. But at the end of the recess

Dalton was replaced by Lyttelton and he withdrew the amendment. A statement was made to the effect that the Board of Trade had 'on very mature consideration' decided to press for the original form of the first schedule. The Friends' amendment was negatived.

The amendment had been attacked by those concerned with industries in West Cumberland. The County Council also pressed for the whole of the Lake District to be in the Development Area. The Ministry of Town and Country Planning did not press for the Board of Trade amendment as they did not feel any need for statutory protection of this kind to preserve the amenities of the Lake District. None the less this episode allowed Symonds to conclude that it was doubtful that National Parks could be planned by conflicting Government Departments or County Councils. Symonds whole-heartedly supported the idea of a National Parks Commission as a 'statutory guardian'. It was necessary for W. S. Morrison, Minister of Town and Country Planning, to attempt to placate Symonds' fears. In a letter of July 1945 he argued that the Lake District was not endangered by the new legislation: 'There is no conflict such as you fear between us and the Board of Trade; we have effective machinery for departmental consultation with them, and this will be directed to upholding the planning ideals which we all wish to see put into practice—namely, the establishment of balanced industrial development in suitable areas, and the pro-tection, unspoilt, of the beauty of the countryside.'

But there were other illustrations of conflicting interests. The case of Shorts' seaplane factory built on the shores of Lake Winder-mere was an example. When it was built, an undertaking was given by the Ministry of Aircraft Production that the factory would be removed 'as soon as the military situation made it safe to do so at the end of the war'. A further undertaking was given by the Ministry of Works that the temporary housing would be removed 'as soon as the housing needs of other parts of the country no longer make advisable the retention of this temporary housing accommodation'. However, in July 1945 Westmorland County Council thought that 'a portion at any rate of the factory and housing estate might well be maintained in being and usefully employed during the reconstruction period'. Symonds, who prepared this dossier, concluded, 'we do not think that, in the four corners of England, a better case can be found to support an argument that if planning powers in National Park areas are not firmly placed in the controlling hands of a National Park Commission, there will be no National Parks'.

The Lake District has been cited as a detailed example of the local authority situation, the new pressures and the sharp advocacy of those groups who regarded themselves as guardians of amenity. Increasingly, the argument was not about the principle of National

Parks, but about their administration. This was the background against which John Dower's Report was prepared.

The Report was a study of the problems relating to the establishment of National Parks in England and Wales, the first comprehensive account since the Addison Report of 1931. Compactly written, it had two parts, the first dealing with the purposes and requirements of National Parks, and the second, much the shorter, relating to the authority for National Parks. In the first part, ten National Park areas were delineated together with other areas which might be considered for possible selection. For the first time there was a national 'shopping list' prepared from informed observation in the field, on which subsequent studies could build. The first part also considered important aspects of principle in the idea of National Parks and criteria against which they should be regarded. Again, the importance of the Report can be seen in its careful explanation of objectives in a National Park programme; in later years many of those engaged in National Park legislation were to go back to this Report for guidance in first principles.

Dower considered that potential National Park areas amounted to some 8,000 square miles in England and Wales. His first list he called *suggested National Parks*, 'those areas which I consider most suitable, and desirable for establishment as National Parks during the first period of operations (say 5 years)':

the Lake District,
Dartmoor,
Pembroke Coast,
Craven Pennines (Wharfe, Aire and Ribble),
Exmoor and North Devon Coast,
Snowdonia,
the Peak District and Dovedale,
Cornish Coast (selected parts),
Black Mountains and Brecon Beacons,
and the Roman Wall.

These areas totalled approximately 3,600 square miles.

His second list contained *Reserves for possible future National Parks*, 'areas which I consider suitable for National Parks, and some at least of which it will be desirable to establish as such at a later stage'. These, amounting to a further 4,400 square miles were:

the Broads,
Dorset Coast and Heaths,
North-east Cheviots (Till and Coquet),
Swaledale Pennines (with part of Wensleydale),
Merioneth Coast and Mountains (including Berwyns),
and the Elenith Mountains (Elan, Towy and Cothi).
North York Moors and Coast,
Berkshire and Marlborough Downs,
North Pennines (South Tyne, Wear and Tees),
Howgill Fells (upper Lune),
Plynlimmon,
Radnor and Clun Forests,

In addition, a third list specified other amenity areas. These included:

Northern :
Northumberland Coast (part),
South-West Cheviots,
Bowland Fells,
Nidderdale Pennines,
Industrial Pennines,
Charnwood Forest,
Cannock Chase,
Delamere Forest.
Western :
Anglesey Coast,
Lleyn Coast,
Denbigh Moors,
Clwydian Range,
Cardigan Coast,
Gower,
The Eppynt,
South Shropshire Hills,
Malvern Hills,
Forest of Dean and Lower Wye.

South-Western :
the Cotswolds,
the Mendips,
the Quantocks,
Cornish Coast (remaining parts),
South Devon Coast,
Blackdown Hills,
Dorset Downs.
Southern and Eastern :
the New Forest,
Hampshire Downs and
    Hindhead,
South Downs,
Forest Ridges (Horsham to
    Battle),
North Downs,
the Chilterns,
Breckland,
Suffolk Heaths and Coast,
and the North Norfolk Coast.

The principles which underlay Dower's approach to National Parks in this country began with his definition of a Park: 'an external area of beautiful and relatively wild country in which, for the nation's benefit and by appropriate national decision and action, (a) the characteristic landscape beauty is strictly preserved, (b) access and facilities for public open-air enjoynfent are amply provided, (c) wild life and buildings and places of architectural and historic interest are suitably protected, while (d) established farming use is effectively maintained' (para. 4).

It stemmed from this definition that 'National Parks should be in a true and full sense *national*' (para. 13). Local interests were not to be disregarded, however, and indeed the well being of their population was to be the first consideration. 'But it does mean that their holiday and recreational use should be for people—and especially young people—of every class and kind ... National Parks are not for any privileged or otherwise restricted section of the population but for all who care to refresh their minds and spirits and to exercise their bodies in a peaceful setting of natural beauty.'

If National Parks were to be provided *for* the nation they should be provided *by* the nation. Dower's conclusion had clear implications. 'Their distinct cost should be met from national funds; the requisite special provisions should be determined by Parliament; and an appropriate national body, under Ministerial and Parliamentary responsibility, should delimit their areas, should direct and supervise all necessary administrative measures for their preservation, access and facilities, and should itself take executive charge where this cannot be satisfactorily undertaken by existing agencies' (para. 14). This was the basis of Dower's subsequent recommendation for a National Parks authority.

Dower underlined these principles by defining two dominant purposes of a National Park. He considered that these should stand supreme out of the numerous possible purposes for which the land might be used and developed. These were '(a) that the characteristic beauty of the landscape shall be preserved, and (b) that the visiting public shall have ample access and facilities within it for open-air recreation and for enjoyment of its beauty' (para. 15).

It is not necessary in this History to summarise all the sections of the Report. Suffice it to say that Dower discussed all the major aspects of the development of National Parks. These included the questions of landscape preservation, conservation and improvement, the farming use of the Parks, recreational facilities, access, footpaths, rambling and water supply, common land and enclosed land, nature reserves and the conservation of wild life, land ownership, the Forestry Commission and the National Trust.

In the second part of his Report Dower considered the type of authority required for National Parks. It should be remembered that he was writing at a time when a number of features of post-war planning were still under consideration. As he acknowledged, until the general machinery and powers for planning had been determined, it was impossible to decide what special machinery and additional powers were needed. Nevertheless, Dower concluded that National Parks (and National Nature Reserves) were important enough and distinct enough to warrant a specific national authority. He emphasised that joint action by national and local authorities was essential and that the National Parks authority should not override the Government Departments or central bodies concerned; collaboration was fundamental for success. Moreover, the new authority should not have the full independence of a separate Government Department. Dower had no doubt that 'it should be responsible to and through a regular Departmental Minister, and ... that the Minister for the purpose should be the Minister of Town and Country Planning' (para. 84). He concluded that there were two alternatives for the form of National Parks authority: 'either a "National Parks *Commission*" under the general responsibility of the Minister of Town and Country Planning, or a "National Parks *Service*" or Sub-Department of the Ministry under the direct charge of the Minister.' Both had precedents from other countries and both were practicable in this country, but of the two, Dower had no hesitation in recommending the Commission.

Dower disagreed with the Scott Committee's Report which had recommended that the National Parks authority should become the *ad hoc* local planning authority for the National Park areas. He emphasised the importance of the local authorities collaborating in the planning of National Parks, and he recommended that the planning authority should be an executive joint committee, composed partly of persons nominated by the National Park authority and partly of representatives of the county and district authorities concerned. He did not specify the proportions in the representation, though this was a highly charged matter for subsequent debate. In this, he went beyond the proposal of the Addison Report of 1931 which was that the planning of National Parks areas be performed in the normal way by the joint action of the local authorities involved. Dower felt that more was needed: 'if the National Parks authority are to carry out their task to public and Parliamentary satisfaction, they must have a direct and first-instance concern in the whole range of planning operations, including not least the case-by-case administration of planning control' (para. 88).

Dower had in mind that the Commission should consist of a Chairman and from six to eight other members serving for a fixed term of years and eligible for re-election. Besides a headquarters staff, each National Park would require its own personnel. What was required was a Commission 'of high standing, expert qualification, substantial independence and permanent constitution, which will uphold, and be regarded by the public as upholding, the landscape, architectural and recreational values whose dominance is the essential purpose of National Parks'. They were to be the 'statutory guardian of the claims of amenity in National Park areas against the many rival claims so powerfully sponsored by statutory bodies' (para. 90). National Parks were recognised as a popular cause: there was political necessity for a specific national body to guarantee them.

For the immediate future it was suggested that the Commission be brought into being in two stages. First, a Preparatory Commission should be appointed to assist the Minister to study and delimit the National Park areas in consultation with the local authorities concerned and to prepare the details necessary for an operative system. Secondly, legislation would be necessary, and a National Parks Bill was advocated. In spite of the two stages recommended for implementation, there was some pressure on the Minister to proceed at once with a National Parks Bill. But other steps were necessary first. As Dower argued privately, fully effective planning control, continuously exercised by an expert Commission, was a *sine qua non* of any worth-while scheme. Development must be prohibited or severely limited, and this must involve compensation, with little, if any, balancing betterment. He felt it was necessary to wait for the new planning legislation.[38]

There had been a good deal of inter-departmental examination of the Report as it was being prepared. In his letter to the Minister when he submitted his Report, Dower referred to the consultations that he had had with officers of various Government Departments and to the fact that his Report reflected some of their suggestions. It is reasonable to assume that Dower's views broadly reflected those of the Department as a whole; at least there is no evidence to suggest that Dower was out of step with his colleagues. It is impossible to record all the 'behind the scenes' activity, but it is particularly interesting to note the different views expressed about the type of authority required for National Parks. The difference of view between the Treasury and the Ministry of Town and Country Planning were forerunners of new obstacles which had to be overcome before the future administration of National Parks could be determined. For example, there was a view within the Ministry (Vincent)[39] that favoured the idea of an independent body dealing with countryside amenities generally rather than National Parks in particular. But the Treasury insisted on the more specific limitation to National Parks; only by concentrating on an independent body under the title of National Parks authority, thereby limiting and defining its scope, could the idea get off the ground.

Dower's Report in drafting stages examined certain financial implications of National Parks. There was Treasury concern over the cost, because there were too many unknowns for a reliable estimate. In the published report Dower thought it could 'safely be said that the cost of a generous and progressive scheme of National Parks, expressed as an average annual charge on the Exchequer, would be measured in hundreds of thousands of pounds rather than in millions'. To meet Treasury points Dower omitted any further detailed estimate in the Report. There were also certain omissions of the function of the proposed Commission in deference to Treasury views. Even so Treasury caution was expressed: Usher of the Treasury wrote to Valentine (M.T.C.P.) on 11 April 1945 'we should like to make it clear that if and when the point is reached at which a permanent commission is to be established we shall wish to scrutinise its proposed functions much more closely'.[40] The whole idea of a Statutory Commission came under close examination. In inter-departmental discussions the Treasury had earlier thought that it might be preferable to create and give certain powers to a semi-independent body supported in part by State grant and partly by private moneys. This alternative did not find favour in the Ministry of Town and Country Planning.

In inter-departmental differences of this kind we should recall the relative youth of the new Ministry and all that implied in terms of inexperience and status, although quite what importance to attach to this is difficult to measure. One suggestion is in an internal Treasury note from Usher to Sir Bernard Gilbert in December 1944[41] which contains a revealing reaction which has significance not only for the history of National Parks but the history of planning generally. There had been Sunday paper references to the forthcoming publication of the Dower Report. Treasury officials thought this to be premature by the Ministry of Town and Country Planning until there had been decisions on the proposals contained in the White Paper, *The Control of Land Use* (1944); it was considered 'another example of this Department's irresponsibility'.

The Minister, W. S. Morrison, was subject to increasing political pressure over the Dower Report. In the House on 18 October 1944 Mr. Mander asked the Minister 'whether he has received the Report of the Committee on National Parks; and if he can state the policy of the Government on the subject'.[42] The Parliamentary Secretary, Henry Strauss, replied that he was not sure what Committee he had in mind, but said that it was hoped to publish soon a report on National Parks prepared by his Department. The very next day the Minister, in reply to another question, confirmed that a report was being considered.

There was a Commons debate on 20 March 1945 on National Parks. Impassionately, Mander asked the Minister 'to take a decision and to make it known and so play some part now in preserving this England for which we have been fighting for the last five or six years'. Other Members, Mr. Hugh Molson and Major Proctor, joined in the pressure for action; the Minister confirmed the Government's desire to preserve special areas in the countryside and to publish the report. A further confirmation of intent to publish was given by the Minister in the House on 25 March, again in reply to a question from Mander.

It was with this background that the Minister presented a Memorandum[43] to the War Cabinet Reconstruction Committee on 7 May. The Memorandum was attached to Dower's Report, and accompanied by another Memorandum[44] by the Secretary of State for Scotland to which was attached the report of the Scottish National Parks Survey Committee, which had been working concurrently with Dower (see page 76). The Minister sought authority to set up, by Order in Council under section 8 of the Ministry of Town and Country Planning Act, 1943, a Preparatory National Parks Commission (as suggested in the Dower Report, para. 92). This proposal had already been critically examined by the Treasury. A memo from Sir Bernard Gilbert to the Chancellor of the Exchequer[45] indicated resistance to the proposal. Commissions under section 8 of the 1943 Act were to assist the Minister in the exercise of his functions; they could be given power to hold land. The Order in Council appointing them required an affirmation resolution in Parliament, too heavy a procedure, it was thought, for a body which was merely going to study a certain matter and subsequently advise the Minister. Another disadvantage of a Preparatory Commission was the presumption that the same people appointed would, in due course, go on to the Commission proper. But when it was known just what the Commission was to do, then it may be found that different people would be required from those who undertook the preparatory work. In the meantime, the argument continued, the Minister should keep as free a hand as possible, and as he had powers to appoint Advisory Committees this would seem the more appropriate instrument for procedure.

At the Reconstruction Committee the Chancellor (Sir John Anderson) duly questioned the appropriateness of the Preparatory Commission. He suggested that the type of Commission contemplated by the 1943 Act was a permanent and executive body, such as the Land Commission, which might operate with some degree of independence of the Minister. But with regard to National Parks there would be questions such as land ownership, about which there might be acute political controversy, and this was work which the Government would wish to be closely and continuously associated. The Minister of Agriculture and Fisheries (R. S. Hudson) doubted whether the time had yet come for a Government move in relation to National Parks. He thought it best not to set up a Commission or publish the Report, but to rely on existing powers of land use control. The Scottish proposals required no Preparatory Commission and relied on the appointment of a Committee for further advice on administrative and financial requirements. In these circumstances the Minister of Town and Country Planning was asked to reconsider his proposal for a Commission.

This he did, but publication of the Report, however, was to proceed. The Reconstruction Committee agreed that Dower's letter to the Minister, in which he referred to discussions with Departmental officers, should be substituted by an explanatory note making it plain that the Government were in no way committed to any of the recommendations made. In this way Dower's Report was shorn of its Departmental status; Dower himself assumed the role of consultant and his work became a personal Report to the Minister. The Committee also suggested that the Minister might state that he had referred the Report to an Advisory Committee which would formulate recommendations for further considerations.

This was not acted upon, but the Minister lost no time in appointing Sir Arthur Hobhouse to chair an appropriate Committee.

The Hobhouse Report

Sir Arthur Hobhouse had the following terms of reference:

(a) To consider the proposals in the Report on National Parks in England and Wales (Cmd. 6628) of May 1945, as to the areas which should be selected as National Parks; and to make recommendations in regard to the special requirements and appropriate boundaries of those areas which should be first selected.

(b) To consider and report on the proposals made in that Report as to the measures necessary to secure the objects of National Parks, and on any additional measures necessary to secure those objects.

(c) To consider and make recommendations on such other matters affecting the establishment of National Parks and the Conservation of Wild Life.

The Minister amplified these terms of reference in a letter to Hobhouse of 18 July.[46] He suggested that the Committee might proceed on a number of assumptions—to which, he took care to state, Government was not yet committed—namely that there were to be National Parks; that an appropriate Central Authority, probably in the form of a Commission, would be set up for their administration; and that there would be a solution to the problem of compensation and betterment. The Minister also suggested what the scope and direction of the Committee's work might be. First, he indicated that the Committee might take the Dower Report (with the caveat that the Ministry and Government were not committed to its conclusions) as a preliminary survey of their field of consideration and as a basis for their work. Second, he advised that the Committee should not enter into direct negotiations with local authorities, but might hear evidence from them. Thirdly, he thought that the Committee should not make recommendations on the details of the legislation required for National Parks, although he would welcome suggestions of a general character. Finally, the Minister indicated that he had further given thought to the question of conservation of wild life and the possible establishment of National Nature Reserves. He proposed that a sub-committee of Hobhouse's Committee might suitably be convened and he suggested names and terms of reference for consideration.

The setting up of the Committee coincided with a change of Government. Lewis Silkin, the new Minister of Town and Country Planning, was soon able to inform the Cabinet as to his views on National Parks, suggesting what priorities might be accorded to new legislation in this direction. In a Memorandum[47] to the Lord President's Committee in August 1945 he expressed the strong view that the establishment of National Parks 'to which the public should have proper access, and where accommodation at a low cost should be provided, should be given a relatively high place in our programme'. New legislation would of course have to await the recommendations of the Hobhouse Committee and the settling of the questions of compensation and betterment. Silkin therefore proposed that the introduction of National Parks legislation should follow close upon his main Town and Country Planning Bill. In the meantime he would exercise his existing powers of control in order to ensure that no development was permitted in any of the areas set out in the Dower Report that was harmful to their future use as National Parks.

The political tide was therefore running strongly in favour of National Parks and much now depended on the deliberations of the Hobhouse Committee. They first met on 1 August 1945; before them were 80 meetings, 17 survey tours and the consideration of written and oral evidence from 60 bodies and individuals.* In evidence outright approval came from a wide range of bodies.[48] The holiday and recreational interests gave enthusiastic support. Professional encouragement came from the Royal Institute of British Architects, the Institute of Landscape Architects and the Town Planning Institute. For the latter, the Dower Report was clearly the last word; their secretary Alfred Potter wrote: 'The members of the Council are familiar with the report on National Parks. . . . It was prepared by a distinguished member of the Institute and the Council find themselves so much in general agreement with it and its recommendations that they consider it would be supererogant for them to add anything to it.'

Caution came from other sources. The County Councils Association wished to safeguard rural, county interests. The National Farmers Union stressed the need to protect farming interests. The Association of Municipal Corporations referred to the problems of water supply and stated that where there was any real conflict of interest, the interests of the water supply authorities should prevail. The British Waterworks Association likewise placed great emphasis on dangers of pollution and the need to protect the purity of important sources of water supply. Other bodies were keen to take the opportunity of promoting their interests. For example, the Royal Automobile Club and the Automobile Association in a joint

---

* With Sir Arthur Hobhouse there were Lt. Col. E. N. Buxton, John Dower, Leonard K. Elmhirst, R. B. Graham, Dr. Julian S. Huxley, Mrs. Lindsey Huxley (who died before the Committee completed its work) and Clough Williams-Ellis. Members appointed later were Prof. R. S. Chorley, Sir William Gavin and Mrs. Gerald Haythornthwaite.

submission objected to the view expressed in the Dower Report (para. 33) that 'walkers constitute the chief section of the public for whom the National Parks are provided and that the only necessary provision for motorists was the creation of a recognised scenic circuit road following the boundary of a National Park'. The motorist lobby did not want to be relegated to the fringes or through routes. There were other similar examples. For instance, the Caravan Club wanted no limitations on their freedom, and the British Canal Union wanted the definition of access to include the right to navigate small boats at will on rivers and lakes.

The Central Landowners Association took the view that the dominant purposes of a Park were the maintenance of agriculture and forestry. As a consequence, the approach to National Park status should be gradual and experimental. The Association could see no justification for vesting in the National Parks Authority any special compulsory purchase powers. Neither could they accept the view that the public should have the right to wander at will: there were 'too many dangers inherent in this proposition'. In oral evidence, Sir Charles Price, a member of the C.L.A. 'did not consider the need for National Parks as urgent as was often suggested'. He thought that in amenity areas the public had already obtained from landowners all the facilities they could reasonably expect.[49]

The Chartered Surveyors and the Land Agents Society submitted a joint memorandum which spoke for a number of vested interests. They too stressed the importance of farming: 'the permanent interests of those who live and work in any of these areas should in common justice be given precedence over the transitory interests of the visitors.' They raised the question of compensation for minerals and referred to the old problems of unrestricted access and sporting rights, which had been previous stumbling blocks to legislation. More fundamentally, they went further than the Central Landowners Association in questioning the whole principle of National Parks. They were 'not averse in principle from the amenities of the country-side being made reasonably available to those who wish to enjoy their beauty and peace, yet the two bodies are not convinced that there is sufficient justification for embarking on a scheme for establishing National Parks as such, which might well defeat the objects desired to be achieved. When large numbers of people visit secluded places of beauty and peacefulness, the places will inevitably lose their charm and appeal. In, at any rate, the majority of areas proposed as National Parks, the public already appear to have the facilities they want, and any attempt to define these facilities in an Act of Parliament might easily mean that the facilities available would be reduced rather than increased'. Their evidence concluded: 'If the Town and Country Planning Acts are made really effective and are

reinforced by effective legislation covering the question of compensation; if the problem of hostel and hotel accommodation is
dealt with in an enlightened manner; and if footpaths and bridleways
are clearly defined and maintained, the case for the creation of
National Parks, involving the country in considerable expense,
falls to the ground.'

This was the most (and, in fact, only) comprehensive objection
to the idea of National Parks. All other bodies accepted the general
principle and merely offered caveats or advice in accordance with
their particular interests, a fact which reflects the widespread public
support which had by now built up in favour of National Parks.
There was caution in some quarters but little weight of sustained
objection. The situation had changed markedly from the 1930s.
Evidence from the agricultural and landowner groups was very
much as expected, but the strength of the opposition had declined.
In many ways the focus of objection had shifted, and the point of
debate now centred on the machinery of administration and
planning.

The administrative aspects of National Parks were a source of
concern to a number of witnesses. In particular, they commented
unfavourably on the creation of yet another body overriding local
authorities or Government Departments. The Chartered Surveyors
thought a National Parks authority 'an addition to bureaucracy
hardly likely to commend itself to the public generally'. The Rural
District Councils Association plainly feared the additional hampering
by officialdom: in their evidence they cited the case of the Dove
Valley in Derbyshire where 'the local Rural District Council has
taken energetic and effective action to preserve the amenities of that
area. They have been successful, but to clasp over the area a National
Park appears to be entirely unwarranted, interfering as it would with
industry and housing'. There were heralds here of a prolonged
anxiety about the form of administration for National Parks.

The Report of the Hobhouse Committee was published in July
1947.[50] The main proposals were in respect of five aspects: the
selection and delimitation of National Parks—Conservation Areas,
and the coast (Chapters 3, 8 and 9); administration—the central
and local organisations (Chapters 4 and 5); access and footpaths
(Chapter 11); planning, management and finance (Chapters 6,
7 and 12); and Nature Conservation (Chapter 10). It is not appropriate in this History to review the Report in detail, but it is necessary
to show, in the context of the main proposals, how the conflicting
views, expressed in evidence to Hobhouse and within the Committee,
were finally resolved.

Selection and delimitation. Hobhouse recommended that twelve
National Parks be declared by annual instalments of four over a

period of three years subsequent to legislation (para. 34). The areas recommended were as follows, in an order which 'takes account of geographical distribution and the need for protection' (para. 36).

First instalment:	Approximate area in sq. miles
The Lake District	892
North Wales	870
The Peak District	572
Dartmoor	392
Second instalment:	
The Yorkshire Dales	635
The Pembrokeshire Coast	229
Exmoor	318
The South Downs	275
Third instalment:	
The Roman Wall	193
The North York Moors	614
Brecon Beacons and Black Mountains	511
The Broads	181
	5,682

Hobhouse was careful to say that the boundaries of these National Parks required a more precise survey. The Report recommended that the precise delimitation should be the first task of the Commission in its operative stage. The Committee had concluded that there should be no attempt to define final boundaries in their Report or in the Bill.

Of Dower's list of ten National Parks (see page 42), Hobhouse omitted one, namely the Cornish Coast, on grounds of the likely administrative difficulties to result from the long, narrow shape of the area to be selected and the separation from its hinterland by an arbitrary boundary. On the other hand Hobhouse now included two areas from Division B of the Dower Report (Reserves for possible future National Parks): these were the Broads and the North York Moors. A further area from Division C (other Amenity Areas) was also included: this was the South Downs, selected because of 'the importance of including at least one National Park within easy reach of London' (para. 39).

Behind this agreed list lay a good deal of the Committee's work; from their first meeting to their last this matter had their attention. Each area had its advocates both within the Committee and outside it. Some were strongly supported: for example the Joint Committee for the Peak District firmly suggested in written evidence that the area be included ('. . . a battleground of its defenders and despoilers for 20 years, the defeat of the Edale steel works project and of the proposal to blast a motor road through the Winnats being examples of organised public effort to protect this area'). The inherent scenic attractions of the area were supplemented by the long-standing interests of the powerful rambling lobby. The Joint Committee was keen to point out that within 60 miles of Buxton lived half the population of England, and as a consequence the area was very vulnerable to defacement from building development, water under-takings, industry, roads, overhead electricity, refuse tipping, forestry and the decay of farming. The Hobhouse Committee noted that the evidence concerning industry confirmed a survey of mineral workings in the Peak District carried out by a geographer, Stanley Beaver.

But the Peak District was never one likely to be omitted from the Committee's list. The internal debate was about the balance of advantage in respect of some others. The Committee had certain criteria in mind; quite apart from the obvious ones concerning landscape attraction, there was agreement that proximity to centres of population was an important factor, and that if possible there should be at least one National Park within easy reach of London. At first the Berkshire and Marlborough Downs were favoured, but arguments in favour of the South Downs ultimately prevailed.

There were divided views about the Broads. Dower held that this area did not fit in with his definition of a National Park and thought it might be more suitable if the motor boat had never been invented. On the other hand Graham and Huxley argued that its inclusion would have great popular support. This view was helped by a note from K. K. Parker, Regional Planning Officer, Cambridge, to the effect that the Broads Investigation Committee were strongly of the opinion that it was essential to set up a central body to control this area, and this could best be done by establishing a National Park. In the end, the inclusion of the Broads owed much to Huxley's insistence. When the third draft of the Report was being circulated in August 1946 Huxley found it necessary to write to Hobhouse from Paris where he was then on U.N.E.S.C.O. business. The Chairman had previously made the suggestion that the Committee might adopt 'twelve National Parks and the Broads', but Huxley wrote, 'I do not feel that I could put my name to a proposal for what makes virtually 13 National Parks, or for one which would include only 12 but leave out the Broads'.[51]

The Dorset Coast and Heaths areas were included in early survey visits, but were never seriously considered for the final list. Instead, the final selection depended very much on the Cornish Coast. The intrinsic merits of the South West were not in dispute; the problem

54

centred on administrative considerations. At first it was thought that there might be objections against the inclusion of Dartmoor: there was the possible opposition of the Duchy of Cornwall, local objection and the fact that large areas were occupied by the Service Departments. But these difficulties were not insuperable and the final problem remained with the coastal areas. There were difficulties about the designation of a coastal strip as a National Park, but, as a precedent Huxley and Dower had argued in favour of the Pembroke coast; it was thought the designation might improve the possibility of evicting the Service Departments.

In September 1946 the final selection was made. By a majority vote, 12 National Parks were to be recommended and, again by majority vote, the Roman Wall was to be excluded. But there was a last minute review of the decision in October; this centred on whether or not the Cornish Coast should be included. Dr. Willatts (Head of Maps Office, Ministry of Town and Country Planning) was asked whether it was still possible to substitute the Roman Wall for the Cornish Coast without delaying the maps. A telephone call to the Ordnance Survey confirmed that it was possible. The Chairman secured Huxley's agreement in Paris. But the Committee remained firm to the previous decision. However, with due regard to the scenic qualities of the area, they felt their Report should make out a very strong case for Cornwall as a conservation area of first class importance no less in landscape value to many National Parks. Pragmatically, they argued that the exclusion of Cornwall from their list would considerably strengthen their recommendation for conservation areas.

The Hobhouse Committee's proposals for the designation of areas of high landscape quality, scientific interest and recreational value, to be known as Conservation Areas, were an 'essential corollary' to their National Parks scheme (para. 227). These areas did not call for the degree of positive management required in National Parks, but it was important for special measures to be taken to preserve their natural beauty and interest. Fifty-two areas were selected. Some fell short of National Park standards in extent or wildness; others which had intensive land uses did not permit freedom of rambling access; others adjoined proposed National Park areas.

The areas were as follows (in square miles).

Northern :
Northumberland Coast (76),
The Cheviot and Rothbury
  Forest (288),
Kielder Moors (401),

North Pennines (635),
Howgill Fells (311),
Silverdale (79),
Forest of Bowland (289),
Nidderdale Moors (329),

Northern (cont.) :
South Pennines (154),
Howardian Hills (58),
Flamborough Coast (18),
Delamere Forest (27).
Western :
Anglesey Coast (76),
Lleyn Coast (34),
Denbigh Moors (146),
Clwydian Range (120),
Berwyn (205),
Plylimmon (520),
Clun and Radnor Forests (474),
Shropshire Hills (192),
Elenith Mountains (484),
Epynt (179),
Cardigan Coast (18),
Gower (48),
South Glamorgan Coast (14),
Forest of Dean and Wye Valley
(232),
Malvern Hills (23).
South Western :
The Mendips (62),
Bideford Bay (51),
Bodmin Moor (95),
Cornish Coast (269),

Isles of Scilly (7),
South Devon Coast (85),
Blackdown Hills and Sidmouth
Bay (212).
Southern :
Dorset Downs, Heaths and Coast
(441),
Cranborne Chase and West
Wiltshire Downs (231),
The New Forest (243),
Isle of Wight Coast (11),
Hampshire Downs (221),
Hindhead (154),
The North Downs (273),
Forest Ridges (132),
Dungeness (50),
The Cotswolds (660),
Marlborough and Berkshire
Downs (435),
The Chilterns (273).
Eastern and Central :
Suffolk Coast and Heaths (128),
Breckland (313),
North Norfolk Coast (44),
Clipsham-Holywell (24),
Charnwood Forest (39),
Cannock Chase (24).

The total area amounted to 9,835 square miles.

Recommendations on National Parks and Conservation Areas still left the special problems of the coast. Early in the Committee's programme[52] J. A. Steers presented a paper on coastal preservation in which he suggested the whole coast of England and Wales should be planned as one unit. The Committee debated whether a separate Coastal Authority of high calibre was necessary, or whether a Coastal Advisory Committee, which would advise the Minister on coastal planning, would suffice. The Report settled in favour of a Coastal Planning Advisory Committee (para. 265).

Administration. There was no shortage of considered views on the question of administration from bodies and persons invited to submit evidence. The advocates of a strong Commission lost no opportunity in stressing its advantages, and those concerned with local government cautiously maintained their freedom of manoeuvre. For the Committee, the focus of debate frequently centred on the size and nature of the Planning Committee which was to be responsible for a particular National Park.

The Standing Committee on National Parks wanted planning in National Parks to be carried out by a special Executive Joint Planning Committee with a majority of members to be appointed by the National Parks Commission and a minority by local authorities.[53] The Committee would be small, but with full planning powers for interim control, and for making and administering a scheme. The chairman and a chief technical officer would be appointed by the Commission. The Standing Committee did not go as far as the Scott Report in excluding local authorities from a share in the planning and management of National Parks, but they did recommend a new, separate agency. Behind this advocacy there lay the fear of the undue influence of local interests on the one hand and of the domination by Government Departments on the other.

The National Trust[54] found in favour of control by a Commission under the Minister of Town and Country Planning. But their main concern was to ensure that the Trust be accorded full representation on this Commission. It advanced strong reasons in support of this claim. The Trust had substantial holdings of land in National Park areas; they had long experience of meeting the need for access and landscape preservation; they had contacts with experts in many of the likely National Park problems; and over the years had built up a degree of mutual trust and confidence with owners and local authorities.

The question of the composition of Park Planning Committees was a thorny one and a variety of formulae was provided. A summary of the arguments was provided by Graham for the Committee in August 1946.[55] The possible variations included the following:

(a) $\frac{2}{3}$ local authority representation and $\frac{1}{3}$ nominated by the Commission and appointed by the Minister. This had been put forward in the Committee's draft Reports.

(b) The proposal of the Standing Committee on National Parks: this was for 'a majority' nominated by the Commission.

(c) $\frac{1}{2}$ local authority and $\frac{1}{2}$ appointed representatives with an appointed Chairman, as suggested by Lord Chorley.

(d) Tripartite membership: one part local authority, one part nominated by the Commission and one part nominated from bodies with interests in National Parks either in equal proportions or $\frac{2}{5}$, $\frac{2}{5}$, $\frac{1}{5}$, respectively. Again, this had appeared in draft Committee Reports.

(e) Sir William Gavin's suggestion of at least $\frac{1}{3}$ local authority representatives, leaving the exact composition to the discretion of the Minister.

(f) The suggestions of Mrs. Haythornwaite and Graham for not less than ⅓ and not more than ⅔ to be appointed by the Minister, the remainder being local authority representatives.

(g) A single Park Committee might appoint a Planning Sub-committee with local authority representatives in the majority, and a Management Sub-committee with Commission representatives in the majority. Sir William Gavin put this forward together with,

(h) all plans and permissions for development emanating from the Park Planning Authority (with a local authority majority) should be subject to endorsement by the Parks Management Committee or the National Parks Commission.

(i) A Park Advisory Planning Committee with local authority representatives in the majority.

In considering these alternatives, Dower made a strong plea for Park Planning Committees with a local authority majority, in order not to cause antagonism. In the event, it was Lord Chorley's 50–50 representation which was finally proposed in the Committee's Report (para. 76). But as we shall see later the matter was by no means concluded and the composition of local Committees was to be a matter of intense concern during the preparation of the 1949 Bill, and for many years afterwards.

Hobhouse recommended Park Committees, with a composition not normally exceeding 25 in number, the chairman to be appointed by the Commission. Local authority representatives should form half, the other half appointed by the Commission and drawn from persons resident within or near the Park, with a local understanding and an appreciation of the wider issues involved. It was proposed that the appointment of the Committee's Planning Officer should be subject to approval by the Commission, and that the Park Committee should assume both planning and management functions.

As to the Commission itself, the attitude of the most important local authority body, the County Councils Association, was important. In a submitted memorandum they agreed in principle to the establishment of a specific national authority. They much preferred a Commission with a high degree of independence to that of a 'service' which would be merely a sub-department of the Ministry of Town and Country Planning. But the independence was not to be absolute. The Minister should be the medium through which Parliamentary oversight of the Commission was exercised, and works carried out by the Commission, which would normally require the consent of the local planning authority, should continue to be so controlled. In the event, the Hobhouse Committee proposed a Commission consisting of a chairman and eight members, each appointed for personal qualifications and not as representatives of any special interests or bodies. It was recommended that the Commission's operations should be financed by the Exchequer and the Commission should be responsible to Parliament through the Minister of Town and Country Planning. The Commission should have an administrative and technical staff.

There was one other aspect of administration to be decided. The Wild Life Conservation Special Committee embraced ideas for National Nature Reserves, Local Nature Reserves and Wild Life Conservation Areas and a Biological Service as an Authority for administering the Reserves. Huxley outlined these ideas at a Joint Meeting between the National Parks Committee and the Wild Life Conservation Special Committee.[56] Dower was opposed to these views on the grounds that they were proposing a wide separation of the two organisations of National Parks and Wild Life Conservation by placing them under different Ministries, to be brought together by co-ordination. Dower advocated one composite National Parks and Nature Reserves Authority. Huxley, however, argued that National Nature Reserves were the essential laboratories of the proposed Biological Service and should not be tied to National Parks, and this argument won the day.

Access and Footpaths. The Hobhouse Committee had been sitting for seven months, when in March 1946 the terms of reference were extended to include consideration of the general law concerning access and rights of way. In July the Minister announced the setting up of a Special Committee on Footpaths and Access, also under the chairmanship of Sir Arthur Hobhouse.

The question of footpaths and access had figured prominently in the Dower Report and received some mention in the Scott Report; before this, the abortive Access to Mountains Act, 1939, had largely been promoted because of the pressures to overcome problems in this connection. The matter was therefore central to the promotion of countryside recreation facilities. Moreover it was timely to re-examine the issues involved. Quite apart from the sitting of the main Hobhouse Committee, there was by this time a good deal of factual information available from the records of an inter-departmental committee on Footpaths and Commons which had been set up to examine proposals in the Scott Report and which had worked until 1944.

The main problems relating to footpaths were twofold: legal provisions for establishing proof of right of way, and liability for upkeep of rights of way. The following paragraphs describe the shortcomings of relevant legislation and the particular issues which demanded attention.

Except where a 'highway' (a term which included footpaths and bridleways) could be proved to have been created under statutory authority, in order to establish proof of a right of way it was necessary to present sufficient evidence to warrant dedication by some owner of the freehold. In fact there were very few formally dedicated footpaths and most of them had been merely trodden out on the ground. Before the passing of the Rights of Way Act, 1932, it was usual in footpaths disputes for the oldest inhabitants to testify that the path in question had been used by the public without hindrance from a time beyond memory. The 1932 Act simplified the procedure by limiting the period of evidence to 20 years uninterrupted public use. But a landowner could close a footpath on his land and place on the public the onus of producing sufficient evidence to warrant the assumption of dedication. When the local authority took no action, the result was that footpaths were lost to the public.

The 1932 Act enabled landowners to submit maps to local authorities indicating those footpaths on their land which they admitted to be rights of way. Occasionally, local authorities made their own footpath surveys. The Scott Committee considered it should be a statutory obligation upon local authorities to record on maps and to signpost clearly all undisputed rights of way. They also recommended a Footpaths Commission with power to investigate all disputed cases and to give decisions. It was in these circumstances that the suggestion of a complete survey of the footpath system of England and Wales was considered.

With regard to the liability for the maintenance of rights of way, the situation was that Parish Councils, under the Local Government Act, 1894, had limited power to repair footpaths (but not bridleways), but were under no legal obligation to do so. County Councils, as highway authorities, were responsible for the repair of highways in rural areas, but the definition of highways did not include footpaths (this was arguable, however, and turned on the interpretation of section 23 of the Highway Act, 1835). But although the wording of the legislation might be ambiguous, the results of the legislation were not, and there was a need to bring all public footpaths, old and new, up to a proper standard and thereafter to maintain it. The Dower Report suggested that this task, as a compulsory duty, should be undertaken by *one* set of authorities throughout the country.

There were a number of other questions concerning access. For example, there was the matter of closure of footpaths, where an important distinction obtained between rural and urban areas. The general procedure for the closure or diversion of footpaths was under the Highway Act, 1835. The procedure was a lengthy one in rural districts, but it did provide an opportunity for objections

60

to a proposed closure, whereas in boroughs and urban districts the safeguards were not so adequate. Other matters which needed to be resolved included signposting, which was inadequately undertaken; the erection of misleading notices, which acted as constraints to access; and the presence of bulls in fields, again a factor which intimidated public access.

With regard to the *creation* of footpaths, new paths could be created by dedication by the owner of the land. Alternatively, the provision of new footpaths was dealt with in planning schemes under the Town and Country Planning Act, 1932. But there was a need for the more creative planning of new footpaths; long-distance, cross-country footpaths, which required some central co-ordination in administration to construct, had been mooted. Well-known proposals included the Pennine Way from the Peak District to the Scottish Border, and the linking up of the old coastguards' paths.

The question of access extended to the complex problem of common land. It had been estimated in the Dower Report (para. 41) that 11% of National Park areas were common land; the total area of common land in England and Wales was thought to be approximately 2,500 sq. miles. The only systematic attempt at survey had been the return prepared by the Copyhold Inclosure and Tithe Commission in 1874, and a new survey of commons was becoming imperative.* This was particularly so if further enclosure was to be prevented and if commons enclosed temporarily during the war were to be re-established to their former use.

The rights of common only applied to certain persons—the commoners—and the general public had no legal right of access unless obtained by statute. In a number of cases the public had a legal right to access to commons; these were commons regulated by schemes under the Metropolitan Commons Acts or the Commons Acts of 1876 or 1899, commons subject to section 193 of the Law of Property Act, 1925, and commons which had been purchased for the purposes of a public open space by a local authority or the National Trust. The total extent of commons regulated under these schemes in 1938 amounted to only approximately 180,000 acres. The most important scheme was that of the 1925 Act. Section 193 gave the public a legal right of access for air and exercise to certain types of common by the owner by deed (though revocable if the owner so wished). The Commons Society for long had suggested that s.193 should be made to apply automatically to all commons, irrespective of action by owners, without prejudice to the subsequent making of a scheme by a local authority. The Dower Report (para. 42) had noted the importance of permanently 'opening' common

---

* This was eventually carried out by the Royal Commission on Common Land, 1955–58.

land in National Park areas, whether by applying this section of the 1925 Act or by some other method of similar effect.

Access to uncultivated land had been a matter which the Access to Mountains Act, 1939, had sought to resolve—inadequately, as we have seen. The Act did not directly confer right of access to any land but provided machinery whereby access to specified areas might be given under Orders made by the Ministry of Agriculture. The Act only allowed a piecemeal approach to securing rights of access; innumerable applications would be necessary and the bulk of the cost of these would fall on voluntary societies.

The many questions relating to footpaths and access were therefore complicated; there was a surfeit of unresolved problems and a necessary reliance on ancient legislation. The Special Committee tackled this field, and the Hobhouse Report only reviewed the situation very generally. The Special Committee's Report[57] contained the recommendations.

They referred to rights of way, long-distance footpaths, and access to land. They are briefly summarised as follows. It was recommended that a complete survey of all rights of way should be undertaken and completed within a period of four years by County Councils and County Borough Councils. In order to settle disputes, Quarter Sessions should form the necessary tribunal. Each Court of Quarter Sessions for a County or County Borough should establish a Rights of Way Committee from its members. They would deal with all applications for closure or diversion of rights of way. Responsibility for repair and maintenance of all rights of way would fall on highway authorities. It was considered that these authorities should be under a general duty to prosecute those obstructing a right of way, while safeguarding certain agricultural practices. Footpaths should be signposted.

It was recommended that proposals for the creation of new rights of way should be initiated by local planning authorities. In particular, the proposals of the National Parks Committee in respect of long-distance footpaths should be implemented, coastal footpaths being the first objective.

With regard to access, the recommendation was that a new measure to provide machinery for obtaining access to uncultivated land was required in substitution for the Access to Mountains Act, 1939. The duty of designating such land should fall on the planning authority, and a procedure for designating 'access land' was outlined. Suggestions were made in respect of conflicting interests in land, but it was thought that all beach and shore should be designated as access land. A 'Country Code' should be published to encourage responsible behaviour in the countryside.

Hobhouse's Special Committee reported in July 1947, 12 months after their appointment; publication came in September. They had held 40 meetings and there had been a further 26 meetings of sub-committees. Written and oral evidence had been considered. As with previous National Parks and related Reports, the Committee had no doubt as to the importance of their proposals. There was almost a messianic flavour to their concluding paragraph, quite in keeping with the National Parks and countryside lobby at this time: 'If our proposals are accepted, and pass into law, they will confer upon the public a precious gift of greater rights and privileges. They will protect and preserve, more simply and yet more adequately than in the past, the footpaths engraved on the face of the land by the footsteps of our ancestors. They will provide long-distance footpaths which may be followed for many miles away from the din and danger of busy motor roads. In the wilder parts of the country our recommendations will provide for the greatest freedom of rambling access consistent with other claims on the land. They will enable active people of all ages to wander harmlessly over moor and mountain, over heath and down, and along cliffs and shores, and to discover for themselves the wild and lonely places, and the solace and inspiration they can give to men who have been "long in city pent". Thus we believe an effective contribution will be made to the health and well being of the nation, and an important step taken towards establishing the principle that the heritage of our beautiful countryside should be held in trust for the benefit of the people.'

Planning, Management and Finance. The Hobhouse Report reviewed the general planning requirements facing the proposed Commission. In this respect the Committee had the advantage of knowing the likely form of the Town and Country Planning Bill and the functions of the new Central Planning Authority. Chapter VI contains little that was exceptional or controversial at the time, but the recommendation in para. 116 is worthy of note in the light of the newly developing planning system and the need for a method of resolving differences between local and central government. This was to the effect that 'a permanent Committee of the Cabinet, or of Ministers, should be set up, and should be charged with the reconciliation of all claims to the use of land by government departments'. A suggestion had been made by the Friends of the Lake District that appeals might be made to a sub-committee of the Cabinet or to a Committee of the Privy Council or preferably to a Joint Committee of the two Houses. The Chairman thought that this aimed to give the Commission the status of a Government Department in any dispute with other Departments, with a system of appeal past the Minister to a super-ministerial body. There was general caution about a special appeal tribunal, but Dower proposed a Standing Committee of the

Cabinet to deal with all inter-departmental questions of the use of land.[58]

A progressive policy of the management of National Parks was outlined in Chapter VII. There are two aspects on which we might comment. The first is contained in para. 195 and related to the great need 'for accommodation providing reasonable comfort and amenities at a price within the reach of moderate incomes'. In the economic climate of the late 1940s this suggestion had little chance of implementation. But it is an interesting reminder of the degree of public management of resources in National Parks which was widely anticipated at this time.

The second concerns the National Trust (para. 184). Hobhouse endorsed the recommendation of the Dower Report that in suitable cases the Commission should have power to transfer land which they have acquired to the National Trust, particularly where the areas in question would be conveniently administered with, or would round off, existing Trust properties. The Trust always regarded that they had a special part to play in the management of land, nationally, for outdoor recreation. In evidence, a certain intransigence of view heralded conflict between the Trust, the Park interests and Government. The Trust in a memorandum submitted to the Hobhouse Committee assumed that in the management of its Estates within National Park areas it would be left unfettered and unhampered by any interference or control. It was claimed that 'the ultimate object of the National Trust and the National Parks Commission are so closely akin that it can be taken for granted that the management of National Trust property will be in accordance with the wishes of the National Park Commissioners'.

George Mallaby, Secretary of the Trust, also submitted a letter after oral evidence was given.[59] He emphasised the unique role of the National Trust in its voluntary subscriptions. The provision of National Parks by the state might be limited by demands on the Exchequer, but the public could do a great deal by supporting the National Trust. Meanwhile the Trust maintained their opposition to one aspect of National Park administration. The Trust was willing to hold and manage land acquired by a National Parks authority, but they could not commit themselves to the general principle of becoming the landlord of all land, without exception, so acquired. There would have to be consultation in each case in order to make sure that the land offered to the Trust came within the definition of its charter.

Chapter XII of the Hobhouse Report contains the principal heads under which financial provision would be needed, and the order of expenditure involved. Four items of capital expenditure totalling £9·25m. over a 10-year period were listed as follows:

	£
1. construction or adaption of National Park buildings and centres	250,000
2. acquisition and improvement of land	5,000,000
3. removal or mitigation of disfigurements in National Parks and Conservation Areas	3,000,000
4. provision of holiday accommodation	1,000,000
	9,250,000

In addition, there would be recurrent expenditure at the initial and fully operative stages of the National Park and Conservation Area scheme totalling £170,000 p.a. initially and £750,000 p.a. ultimately. We shall see in a later section how these estimates compared with actual expenditure.

Nature Conservation. The question of Nature Conservation was taken up by the Wild Life Conservation Special Committee, and their recommendations were contained in the Huxley Report, *Conservation of Nature in England and Wales*, 1947 (Cmd. 7122). With the setting up of the Nature Conservancy (the national Biological Service proposed by the Special Committee) this particular area of concern became separated from the National Parks movement generally. Accordingly, it is not examined in this chapter of the Official History.

.   .   .

The Hobhouse Report concluded with the belief that 'we have set out a scheme for the protection of landscape beauty and the encouragement of open air recreation in the wild and unspoilt country of England and Wales which will be a great national investment, yielding unlimited returns in health and happiness, in opportunities for the enjoyment of country pursuits and interests, and in a new growth of understanding between town and country'. Legislation was the next step, and in the next two years slow progress on a National Parks Bill showed how difficult it was to translate these high hopes into effective provision. In Scotland, indeed, the expectations were to be thwarted, and it is to this special case that we first turn.

CHAPTER 4

The Situation in Scotland to 1947

THE National Parks movement in Scotland took root relatively slowly, exhibiting little of the vitality in the later 1930s that was a feature in England and Wales. Scotland had been represented on Sir Christopher Addison's National Parks Committee, which reported in 1931 (see page 14), by Sir Robert Grey and Sir John Stirling-Maxwell. The Committee, recognising that Scotland required special consideration, recommended the establishment of a separate Scottish authority to deal with National Parks. No steps were taken to implement that report, but there were a number of isolated ventures which were in keeping with the National Park idea. These were undertaken by Glasgow Corporation, the Forestry Commission and by the National Trust. As early as 1906 the Ardgoil Estate was given to Glasgow Corporation by Mr. Cameron Corbett, and in 1936 these 7,000 acres were combined with adjacent lands of the Forestry Commission; the total area of 54,000 acres (84 sq. miles) became known as the Argyll National Forest Park. Much the greater proportion of this tract, and particularly that part above 900 ft., was subject to no restrictions on public access. The Forestry Commission had other areas, such as Glen Trool in the south and Queen's Forest in the Cairngorms. Another tract of fine mountain country, again available to climbers and hikers, was purchased in 1937 by the National Trust for Scotland; this was the Balness Estate in Argyll, 11,600 acres in extent.

At the outbreak of war, the Scottish situation was appreciably different from that of England. There was only one major conurbation, Clydeside, and population pressure on the countryside in no way compared with, for example, the situation in the London area or parts of the North. Furthermore, there was already some significant hill and mountain country with no restrictions on public access. Elsewhere, however, there were strong sporting interests which precluded ready access to open land. The Access to Mountains Act, 1939, did not apply to Scotland because it had not been possible to obtain a reasonable measure of agreement on the part of the Scottish organisations concerned. The nature of pressure for change was not strong enough to break vested interests to maintain the status quo. A Scottish Footpaths Bill prepared by the Scottish Rights of Way

Society was not regarded as acceptable by the Government because of the controversial nature of its proposals.

However, enthusiasm for National Parks extended to Scotland during the wartime years, influenced by a quickening climate of expectation in England and Wales. In spite of early resistance and apathy the Scottish authorities became caught up in studies on the lines of the Dower Report and committees of the Hobhouse type.

The Scott Committee, appointed in October 1941, gave the first opportunity in Scotland for raising a number of issues concerned generally with the countryside. In August of that year, when Lord Reith's proposal for the Committee was becoming known, H. G. Vincent of the Ministry of Works and Buildings was in touch with the Department of Agriculture in Scotland (R. G. Hattle): would it be the wish to extend the enquiry to Scotland? The reply (from J. M. Caie) declined the invitation on the grounds that the Secretary of State had in mind to set up an Advisory Council on planning in Scotland which would almost certainly be considering the question of the establishment of rural industries. 'It would be manifestly undesirable that there should be two bodies studying the same subject,' he wrote.[60] This decision was not reversed.

The Scott Report in 1942 (para. 241) acknowledged that Scotland was outside the Committee's terms of reference. The Committee considered, however, 'that whatever degree of autonomy Scotland may have within the scheme, a national plan must make provision for the whole of Britain. The great problems of Scotland, such as the future of the Highlands, are enormous problems which ought to be faced by a united nation. Scotland lies wholly outside Britain's central belt of growing industry and population and seems likely to suffer continued depopulation and migration of industry if the planning for Scotland is carried on independently.' But this plea failed to arouse any great enthusiasm for the Report in the Scottish Office. The recommendations on footpaths and the proposal for a Footpaths Commission caused as much interest as any, and these were referred to the newly founded Scottish Council on National Parks for further exploration (see p. 70). But official reaction was bleak, and the end of the matter came with correspondence between Sir Horace Hamilton (Under Secretary of State for Scotland) and the Lord Advocate in October 1942. The Lord Advocate commented, 'I will only say that the Report appears to me to provide magnificent ammunition for those who distrust ambitious planning, and I do not envy you if you have to try to find practicable schemes for carrying out some of the recommendations'.[61] He said he had difficulty in understanding how the proposed Footpaths Commission would work in Scotland; it was already the duty of Town and County Councils under s.42 of the Local Government (Scotland) Act, 1884, to assert and keep open any rights of way which the public have acquired by grants, subscription or otherwise.

In November the Secretary of State (T. Johnston) was asked in the House to state his intentions in the light of the Scott Report. He was asked by Mr. Henderson Stewart* whether he would consider setting up a committee to report on land utilisation in Scottish rural areas. The answer given was that a new body for this purpose was not desirable. Committees had already been appointed to consider many subjects of vital importance to the Scottish countryside—for example, hill sheep, land settlement, hydro-electric development and the herring industry. Advisory committees on housing and education had been reconstituted and they would review conditions in the country as well as the town. Furthermore, the Scottish Council on Industry would concern itself with the establishment and maintenance of rural industries.

But the Secretary of State had a change of heart. The reasons for this are obscure, but the facts are that he set up a small committee in January 1943 to review the steps that were being taken in Scotland to ensure that the recommendations of the Scott Report, as far as applicable to Scottish conditions, were receiving proper attention. This was a significant departure from his previous statement; perhaps it was motivated by a sense of political caution or actually to stifle a particular pressure for a committee with wider terms of reference, such as had been requested of him earlier. The Chairman of his Committee was Lord Normand, Lord President of the Court of Session. The members were: Col. the Hon. Ian G. Campbell, District Commissioner for the Northern Civil Defence District and a person with an intimate knowledge of conditions in the Highlands; Hector McNeill, a member of Glasgow Corporation and Deputy District Commissioner for the Western Civil Defence District; and Sir John Milne-Home, Vice-Convenor of Dumfries County Council, Chairman of the Dumfries Agricultural Executive Committee and a member of the Scottish Agricultural Advisory Committee.

The Committee worked rapidly and presented its short report in May 1943: *Utilisation of Land in the Rural Areas of Scotland.*† Their finding was that 'on the evidence submitted to us, we are satisfied that the recommendations of the Land Utilisation Committee have all been scrutinised and that most, including all the more important and urgent of them, are now being given close and practical study'. An unpublished appendix[62] to the Normand Report summarised the ways in which the Scott proposals were being acted upon. With regard to Nature Reservations, a Scottish Nature Reserves Committee had been established. As to access to the countryside, the

* 17 November 1942.
† Report of Committee, Scottish Office, Cmd. 6440.

Scottish Home Department had an interest in the tourist industry and was in touch with the Scottish and U.K. voluntary associations concerned. With regard to National Parks, the recommendation was being considered by the Department of Health, the Department of Agriculture and the Scottish Education Department, all of whom had been in touch with the Scottish Council on National Parks. Additionally, it was understood that the Forestry Commissioners intended to increase the number of National Forest Parks.

The Scottish Council were in fact about to meet the Secretary of State, and it is to this body and its influence that we should now briefly turn. The Council owed its origin to the initiative of the Association for the Preservation of Rural Scotland (A.P.R.S.) which had convened a conference in Edinburgh in January 1942 to consider the matter of National Parks and to set up a standing National Parks Committee for Scotland in order to draw up a policy for their provision and administration. There was a large attendance with representatives from 30 societies concerned with open air life or rural amenities, three Government Departments (Agriculture, Health and the Forestry Commission), the Association of Counties and Cities in Scotland, and the Carnegie U.K. Trust. The Conference resolved to form the Scottish Council. The main argument was that Scotland owed much to the provisions made by the Forestry Commission and the National Trust, but more was now needed, and there could be no single reliance on the efforts of the past.

The Council considered the question of National Parks during 1942, and in February 1943 their President, Lord Keith, forwarded to the Secretary of State a lengthy memo which argued the case for National Parks. It followed familiar arguments, long used by their English counterpart, the Standing Conference, on the lines of community benefits: for example, it believed that 'National Parks are bound to develop not only health giving habits but also mental and moral qualities in the nation'. It also argued on the basis of democratic rights and the need to preserve the countryside from alien development: 'Not least among the advantages would be the feeling that enjoyment was being had as a right rather than as a privilege and the protection that would be given against undesirable development in beautiful surroundings.'[63] The memo advocated a Scottish National Parks Commission and spelled out some of the administrative steps that might be taken within a National Park. Fishing rights, for example, would pass to the Park Authority, and the memo contemplated the extinction of shooting rights within a National Park.

There was no great enthusiasm for this memorandum in the Scottish Office. The reaction at most was cautious. A note by the Department of Agriculture commented that the Scottish Council's proposals meant 'yet another more or less autonomous executive body in the field of buying, owning or using land in Scotland'.[64] Another view that was expressed was the dislike of leaving the Forestry Commission in the position of running National Parks. Their business was seen as afforestation and their function limited to the acquisition or use of land allotted to the purpose. It is impossible to say how widespread this antipathy was towards the Forestry Commission, but it was certainly to reappear with some force. It may be that the Scottish National Parks movement at this time owed a good deal to this defensive apprehension of the Forestry Commission and its growing influence.

The Scottish Council drew up a number of proposals, but these could easily be countered. A National Parks Commission of ten members was requested, set up by the Secretary of State, to represent forestry, farming, architecture, civil engineering, the law and bodies interested in the preservation of wild life and in National Parks. The Department of Health's observations were that this was premature; Scotland might only need two or three National Parks. Another proposal was that the Commission would survey and map land to be scheduled for preservation. The Scottish Office foresaw conflict with hydro-electric interests. The Commission would have the power to compulsorily acquire land, to develop the Parks and to appoint wardens and rangers. (The practical realism of this was called into question.) The Commission should receive an annual grant of £100,000 during their first ten years. (The difference in financial support from the Addison Report was noted, which in 1931 contemplated a grant of £100,000 a year for five years for the whole of Great Britain.) The Commission would delegate forestry work in National Parks to the Forestry Commission. (Difficulties would arise in having two Commissions responsible for certain activities within National Parks.) Lastly, the Commission should be given control over the care and maintenance of all Scottish rights of way. (The Lord Advocate had already pronounced on this question.)

Lord Keith led a delegation to the Secretary of State and Departmental representatives on 15 March 1943. There was an exchange of views about the Council's proposals and the difficulties which surrounded them. The Secretary of State said that it was common knowledge that the Government welcomed the idea of National Parks, but there was a number of difficulties to consider. He was afraid that there might be too many Commissions owning land after the war; he was doubtful as to the reaction to another nominated, non-elective Commission; he thought a right to veto development would meet with opposition from the planning authorities. However, when the survey of areas in England and Wales then being undertaken (by John Dower) was available he said he would consult with the Council again on the possibility of making a similar survey in Scotland.

This was a cautious and non-committal outcome to the meeting. Options for the future were kept open. But the Secretary of State could not be but aware of the increasing influence of the National Parks and amenity lobby. For example, the Hydro-Electric Development (Scotland) Bill was provoking adverse comment from National Park interests. Although the Scottish Council had made no pronouncement, the corresponding English body, the Standing Committee on National Parks, had made representations and representatives were to meet the Secretary of State later that month.* Previously, the Friends of the Lake District had protested to W. S. Morrison, the Minister of Town and Country Planning. The Secretary, Rev. Symonds, had written that the Government's policy was, 'by a state guarantee of the public loan funds of a new board, to provide electric power at rates cheap enough to tempt large-scale industries to establish factory areas in the glens: in other words to multiply Kinlochleven by 70 plus some unknown addition. In effect the policy is to give a (potential) subsidy to a non-profit earning Board, in order that powerful industrial groups may then earn private profit in a place where they ought not to be, and where, but for the Bill, they would not be.'[65] The Secretary of State however was not to be stampeded in giving much away to the Scottish Council at this time.

By November 1943 a draft of the Dower Report was in Scottish hands. It was clear that the Ministry in London was going to take some time to fully consider it and therefore it could not yet be referred to the Scottish Council, as promised. But surprisingly the question of a Scottish survey was reopened. The reason for this seems largely concerned with a difference of opinion with the Forestry Commission during October of that year. Sir Roy Robinson of the Forestry Commission appointed a Committee under the chairmanship of Sir John Sutherland, a former Forestry Commissioner, to advise the Commission on the steps which might be taken to form a National Forest Park in Glen Trool, where 40,000 acres had been leased from the Earl of Galloway. Tom Johnson, Secretary of State, was upset by this, taking the view that he was responsible for planning. Tactically, he recognised that he had promised to negotiate later with the Scottish Council, and they might feel that the Forestry Commission had stolen his thunder. He went to the length of complaining to the Lord President of the Council, C. R. Attlee: 'I think it is all most unfortunate that developments should be going on here outside the control of the Planning Ministers. I quite

* 17 March 1943.

72

appreciate the special interest which the Forestry Commission have in their property, but surely if a venture of this kind which raises important planning questions is projected it is appropriate that the responsible Planning Minister . . . should be in on the ground floor. . . .'[66]

The upshot was that the Secretary of State invited representatives of the Scottish Council to a meeting on 13 December 1943 to discuss the question of a survey of possible National Park areas and to see how National Forest Parks fitted in with National Parks policy generally. Events moved quickly and a Scottish National Parks Survey Committee was appointed in January 1944 to advise on those four or five areas in Scotland which might be suitable for National Parks and to supervise a survey of potential areas. The Committee was not invited to deal with the question of administration or cost of National Parks. Sir Douglas Ramsay of the Scottish Council, and one of H.M. Commissioners for the Balmoral Estates, was Chairman. Other members were: Mr. Peter Thomsen, also of the Scottish Council; Dr. Fraser Darling, the naturalist; and Mr. D. G. Moir, honorary secretary of the Scottish Youth Hostels Association. Dr. Arthur Geddes of the Department of Health acted as Survey Officer. The Scottish Council had played its part in the discussions which led to the setting up of this Committee. The Council remained in being but never assumed the importance of the English Standing Conference as a major source of pressure for change. Instead, for the next few years the future of National Parks in Scotland was very much in the hands of Government Committees.

The Ramsay (Scottish National Parks Survey) Committee met ten times between February and August 1944; it took evidence and members surveyed a number of possible park areas.[67] The work of the Committee proceeded as follows: selection of criteria for National Parks; tentative selection of areas for investigation; consideration of submitted evidence; factual surveys and reports on each area; selection of the most suitable areas; and preparation of a report.

The Committee was helped in the selection of areas by a list previously prepared by the Association for the Preservation of Rural Scotland. This included: the Cairngorms, Cuillins, Glen Affric, Loch Maree, Black Mount-Glencoe, Glen Garry-Glen Quoich, Glen Lyon-Lawers, the Trossachs, and Glen Trool. In November 1943, the Scottish Council had revised and shortened this list to: Glen Affric, Loch Lomond, Black Mount, Cairngorms, Moidart-Morar, and Loch Maree. To this list Dr. Geddes now suggested Arran, Glen Clova-Glen Esk and St. Mary's Loch, the last two serving the needs of Edinburgh and Dundee. The Ochils and Fintry Hills were considered, but there were doubts as to whether they had the requisite scenic quality. The Cuillins were omitted from further consideration because it was felt they were not in danger of being spoiled, and were of limited recreational interest. With regard to Glen Cova-Glen Esk, the boundaries were difficult to define. The best scenic interest was in the north, where it was Royal property and where there were strong agricultural interests; Dundee, it was thought, would be better served by a National Park in Perthshire. On Arran, most of the land was under one owner who had been able to protect amenities without restriction of access, and this was another area deleted from consideration. The Island of Rhum was thought to be suitable as a nature reserve only. After due consideration, field surveys were made of nine areas, as follows:

St. Mary's Loch
Glen Affric-Glen Cannich-Strath Farrar
Loch Lomond-Trossachs
Glen Lyon-Ben Lawers
Ben Nevis-Glen Coe-Black Mount
Moidart-Morar-Knoydart
Loch Torridon-Loch Maree-Loch Broom
The Merrick-Glen Trool
The Cairngorms.

A number of criteria determined this list: outstanding scenic beauty, accessibility, preservation and preservability, recreation facilities, educational, cultural and social interests, flora and fauna, and accommodation. The relative weight attached to the criteria is shown in the surveys given as an Appendix to the submitted Report, but there was some difference between the criteria as published and those that appeared in the Committee's minutes. There is a distinct impression for example that the Committee in their meetings placed some emphasis on the question of land acquisition, but this is not quite so apparent in their Report. For example, the Committee thought that, with regard to the Black Mount-Glen Coe-Ben Nevis area, it was 'difficult if not impossible to find elsewhere in Great Britain a clearly defined area of similar size where a National Park, easily accessible to all could be established with less trouble and expense. The whole northern part belongs to the British Aluminium Company. A large part to the south belongs either to the National Trust for Scotland, Forestry Commission or Department of Agriculture for Scotland. The acquisition of the remaining few miles of deer forest should present no great obstacle.' Accordingly it was recommended as a first selection. What appears in the Report (page 12–13) omits the point about acquisition.

A number of bodies in particular submitted helpful evidence to the Committee. The Clyde Valley Regional Planning Advisory Committee suggested a National Park in the Loch Lomond-Trossachs area. The Scottish Council submitted maps and details of five areas. Specialist authorities such as the Geological Survey and the Ecological Society offered evidence of a technical nature. The most comprehensive evidence was submitted by the Educational Institute of Scotland, with an ambitious list of possible areas. It is remarkable that no bodies were in disagreement with the idea of National Parks in principle, although caution was registered by the Highland Development League and the Scottish Land and Property Federation. The latter confessed to 'considerable hesitation in suggesting without the approval of the owners the conversion of any particular area of land into a National Park or Parks. They would like however to make it clear that they accept the general impression that it is desirable to establish a National Park or Parks.'

The Committee's Report was submitted in October 1944. Mr. Peter Thomsen died in September shortly after the last meeting in August. Of the total of nine areas surveyed, the Merrick-Glen Trool area was finally omitted on the grounds that the Forestry Commission were proposing to set up a National Forest Park there. The following areas, in order of priority, were recommended as suitable for National Parks:

		Approximate area in sq. miles
1.	Loch Lomond-Trossachs	320
2.	Glen Affric-Glen Cannich-Strath Farrar	260
3.	Ben Nevis-Glen Coe-Black Mount	610
4.	The Cairngorms	180
5.	Loch Torridon-Loch Maree-Little Loch Broom	500
		1,870

Mr. Thomsen submitted a minority report in respect of area No. 2. He argued that the Glen Garry-Glen Morriston area be also included in this National Park, on the grounds that scheduling this area a Nature Reserve alone would have no protective value against its invasion or destruction of its natural beauty, such as by hydro-electric projects. A further three areas were placed on a reserve list for consideration at a later date:

		Approximate area in sq. miles
6.	Moidart-Morar-Knoydart	410
7.	Glen Lyon-Ben Lawers-Schiehallion	140
8.	St. Mary's Loch	180
		730

The Committee further recommended that within these areas certain parts should be set aside as Nature Reserves, and that elsewhere, three small areas should be so scheduled, namely the lower reaches of the Garry and the Morriston (see Mr. Thomsen's note of reservation) and the Black Wood of Rannoch. The Report was published as *National Parks: a Scottish Survey,** in the same format as the Dower Report.

At this point the English and Scottish National Parks movements came together. Activity in Scotland had been late in getting under way and it never seemed to have that broad pressure with influence in high places that characterised the English situation, but considerable progress had been made. The question of National Parks was now national in scope, and proposals for England and Wales and Scotland could now be compared and considered together.

The War Cabinet Reconstruction Committee on 7 May 1945 had before them both the Scottish Report and the Dower Report. It will be recalled (see p. 47) that the Minister of Town and Country Planning wished to establish a preparatory National Parks Commission for England and Wales, but he was persuaded that a Committee was the right instrument for further progress at that stage. The Secretary of State's Memorandum was on different lines.[68] 'If the Committee approve the proposal . . . for the establishment of a preparatory National Parks Commission for England and Wales, I would seek approval to the appointment of a Scottish Committee (the Ramsay Committee with added members) to advise me on the administrative and financial requirements of a national parks system in Scotland. My reason for preferring a Committee and not a Commission in Scotland at present is that, as we already have the Ramsay Committee, we ought to make use of their knowledge and experience for the preparatory work.' (The Minister did not have this advantage: the Dower Report was the product of one person, although there had been access to many minds, and an English Committee suitable for continuation did not exist.)

The Secretary of State's proposal was agreed and he invited Sir Douglas Ramsay to chair a newly appointed National Parks Committee, with the following terms of reference:

(a) to consider and report on the administrative, financial and other measures necessary for the provision, on the lines recommended in the Report of the Scottish National Parks Survey Committee, of National Parks in Scotland, and
(b) to consider and make recommendations on such other matters

---

* Report by the Scottish National Parks Survey Committee, Cmd. 6631, H.M.S.O., 1945.

relating to National Parks and on the conservation of wild life as may be referred to the Committee by the Secretary of State for Scotland.

The other members were: Mr. J. M. Bannerman, a member of the Forestry Commission; Col. the Hon. Ian G. Campbell, Nairn County Council, who had served on the Normand Committee in 1943; Mr. George Cruickshank, former County Clerk of East Lothian; Mr. Fraser Darling, naturalist, a member of the first Ramsay Committee; Mr. Robert Grieve, senior technical assistant to Professor Patrick Abercrombie with the Clyde Valley Regional Planning Advisory Committee; Mr. David Howatt, Director of Education, Perth and Kinross; Mr. A. Fraser Macintosh, Aberdeen Town Council; Mr. D. G. Moir, another former member of the Ramsay Committee; Rev. Thomas M. Murchison, Highland Development League; Professor James Ritchie, Chairman of the Scottish Nature Reserve Committee; and Mrs. Jean Roberts, Glasgow Corporation.

The Committee was appointed in January 1946. The first meeting was held in February when the Chairman advised that the Committee might work to three assumptions, similar to those of the English Hobhouse Committee. They might assume that there were to be National Parks; if appropriate, a central authority would be set up for their administration; and that there would be a solution of the problem of compensation and betterment.

Also, a Scottish Wild Life Conservation Committee was appointed, with the chairman Professor Ritchie. The terms of reference were 'to consider and to advise the Scottish National Parks Committee as to the steps which it is desirable and practical to take to conserve wild life in Scotland'. Compared with the English situation, the question of footpaths was not a problem and no special committee was set up to consider this aspect.

The Committee held 18 meetings. Evidence was taken and considered; field surveys were undertaken. The Committee worked closely in parallel with the Hobhouse Committee, and the technical officers kept in contact with the respective deliberations. The Committee operated smoothly, apparently with no discord, and there was little difficulty in coming to generally accepted views. One difference in particular from the Hobhouse Committee was the relative ease with which the Ramsay Committee came to agreement over the role of a National Parks Commission and its relationship with local interests. The relative lack of concern over local versus central powers, compared with the English situation, was striking. Another difference in the working of the two Committees was that relatively little time was spent in Scotland on the consideration of areas for inclusion in the National Park System. The previous

Ramsay Committee had done its work here, and its conclusions were accepted as the base for further work.

Of the views submitted to the Committee, we might note three documents that embraced significantly different approaches.[69] The Scottish Council for National Parks was a strong advocate of public ownership, describing it as 'the natural conception associated with a national park'. The Council went on to make it clear that there would be exceptions to the principle of total land ownership, such as farms, small holdings, and small private ownerships, but even so they went further than anyone else in this direction. It led them to the view that it was essential that private sporting rights be abolished.

The observations of the Scottish Land and Property Federation were expectedly cautious. They made three points: the extent of the demand for National Parks by potential users was not and could not be known; the conversion of an area to a National Park was bound to depreciate—perhaps to extinguish—its value as a sporting subject, and so to affect the local economy; and while generally agreeing with the principle, they thought that National Parks should be created gradually as the demand proved the need.

The evidence of the Association of County Councils in Scotland had an administrative bias. They stressed for example the importance of local committees. With a cautious eye on demands on local rates they recommended a national fund to meet the administrative and development costs of each area.

A general picture of requirements was built up from the submitted recommendations. A Government sponsored central administrative body should be established, supplemented by some form of local organisation (though there were different views as to whether this should be advisory or executive). The National Trust wanted a Director for each Park. With regard to planning, the Town Planning Institute and the Town and Country Planning Association advocated Regional Statutory Planning Authorities with local authority and National Park representatives. The Association of County Councils wanted the local committees to have an adequate planning staff and to be represented on Planning Committees of adjoining areas. The Scottish Council wanted the Commission to be exempt from planning control. Concerning management and development there was general agreement that the Central Authority should control policy, finance and the overall supervision of National Parks. With regard to finance, the Town Planning Institute, the Association of County Councils, the Educational Institute and the Town and Country Planning Association wanted the National Parks system to be financed by the Exchequer. On the other hand the Land and Property Federation thought that Parks should be largely self supporting through entrance, car park and camping fees. There was general agreement that the National Park authority should control sporting rights and should provide suitable camping and caravan sites at reasonable charges.

The Committee's Report[70] was submitted in July 1947 together with that of the Scottish Wild Life Conservation Committee. The Committee had successfully kept in step with Hobhouse. In the light of the general climate of expectation about National Parks affairs at this time, the Report was uneventful with recommendations largely to be anticipated. A National Parks Commission for Scotland should be established, to consist of a Chairman and six other members appointed by the Secretary of State, on a full- or part-time basis. There should be a local Committee for each Park, consisting of 12–18 persons, two-thirds of whom should be representatives of the existing local planning authority(ies) and one-third of representatives of the Commission. (When this matter was considered in Committee there was some concern that the Commission would have their powers whittled away with this minority representation.[71] This point was answered at the time by the explanation that the Commission would not be subject to local planning control of their own land. In fact, the machinery finally proposed was not to work quite like this, and the Report recommended that the Park Planning Committee should have all the powers and duties of a planning authority, but that the Commission should prepare a general plan for the area and submit the plan to the Committee for approval.)

With regard to management, the Commission would be concerned with the preservation of natural amenities; the provision of access, holiday accommodation and recreation facilities; and the maintenance of the continuity of rural life and the fostering of suitable rural industries. It was recommended that land required for specific National Park purposes should generally be acquired by outright purchase. All possible measures should be taken to secure the necessary improvement of means of access (including footpaths) to, and within the Park.

Capital costs of £3¼ millions for National Park development were estimated as:

	£
acquisition of land and compensation	1,500,000
development	500,000
holiday accommodation and recreation facilities	750,000
National Park houses and other buildings	500,000
	£3,250,000

These costs were to be met out of the National Land Fund.

It was assumed that the five areas on the priority list of the Scottish National Parks Survey Committee would be established as National Parks as soon as possible. Further detailed surveys by the Commission would however be required. At the Commission there should be a Chief Executive Officer, designated Director General, and there should also be a Chief Planning Officer. (In Committee there were some who favoured the view that the Chief Executive Officer should be a Commissioner, but this idea was lost on a show of hands.) Each Park should be under the control of a Park Director, and his staff would include a Land Officer.

The Report contained an Addendum, signed by eight members of the Committee, 'Suggestions for Planning a National Park as applied to the Glen Affric area'. This illustrated the application of the general planning recommendations, contained in the Report, to a particular area. This Addendum was the subject of the only real controversy in the Committee. The Chairman and a minority of the membership was against its inclusion on the grounds that it went beyond the remit of the Committee. A compromise suggestion was to have this part of the Report as an Addendum (rather than an Appendix), and signed only by those who agreed to its inclusion.

There were some important differences from the Hobhouse recommendations. For example, the Scottish Commission was seen rather differently from that proposed for England and Wales; it was to be an executive body with a local Committee in each Park to which some executive responsibility might be devolved. In the actual operation of the new system the Committee envisaged a rather greater measure of collaboration between the Commission and the local planning authorities and other agencies (for example the Forestry Commission) than contemplated by the English Committee. There were no recommendations regarding Conservation Areas and the Committee had not dealt with the general question of access to the countryside. The Scottish problem was in fact significantly different from that in England and Wales; it was not merely a question of the conservation and protection of land for public use, but also the development and rehabilitation of the park areas by the encouragement of suitable rural industries and of more adequate facilities for tourists.

But the similarity to Hobhouse was that the Ramsay Committee embraced a clear conviction as to the necessity of National Parks and a belief that their recommendations would provide an effective operational system. One set of proposals largely came to fruition; the other did not. The recommendations in respect of Scotland fell by the wayside; precisely how this happened is shown in Chapters 5 and 8.

CHAPTER 5

The National Parks and Access to Countryside Act, 1949

THE question of National Parks and access to the countryside was now a matter for political will; the appointed Committees had done their work. For a number of years the Government had indicated that National Parks legislation would be prepared and this matter was now in their hands. This chapter examines the period between 1947 and 1949 when the nettle was finally grasped in respect of England and Wales.

The period falls into two phases, first up to mid-1948, and second, from then to the publication of the Bill and its passage through the House. In the first period, after the publication of the Hobhouse Report we look at the early reactions of the Minister (Lewis Silkin), the Ministry (Town and Country Planning) and the Treasury. We also note the continuing attempts of the principal pressure groups to influence thinking on the nature of the proposed Commission, and the arrangements for local administration. We examine the role played by two interested parties, the Standing Committee of the Councils for the Preservation of Rural England and Wales (C.P.R.E. and C.P.R.W.), and the County Councils Association (C.C.A.). In the second period, we note the discussions between Government Departments during the preparation of draft legislation, the continued observations and pressures from different interest groups, and the outcome of important meetings, particularly of the Lord President's Committee.

Phase One, to mid-1948

The Minister. The interest shown by the Minister, and his commitment to the idea of the creation of National Parks was of great importance. In this History it is impossible to evaluate precisely the influence exerted by the Minister, as compared with the Treasury, his own Department's officers or other colleagues such as the Lord President. None the less there is sufficient evidence to suggest that it was the Minister's personal dedication and drive that were largely responsible for positive decisions in favour of National Parks legislation in the early stages of the campaign. We should recall that Silkin had no seat in the Cabinet; his influence and success at this time is all the more remarkable.

Even before the publication of the Hobhouse Report Silkin was pressing for an Amenities Bill in view of the early need to deal with the problem of advertisements.[72] That matter was taken up in the Town and Country Planning Bill but it still left the specific questions of footpaths and National Parks, and as early as February 1947 Silkin wished to stake out a claim for an Amenities Bill in the legislative programme. Support was given by Sir Bernard Gilbert at the Treasury in spite of the uncertainty surrounding the National Land Fund. (It was believed that the Chancellor had in mind legislation enabling land to be acquired compulsorily for the purposes of the Land Fund and that he was thinking of using it in part to acquire National Parks and coastal areas.)

There were two principal questions which the Minister had to consider. One was whether legislation was necessary at all; another was, if so, what should be the provisions. For the past few years the National Parks lobby had seemed to carry universal support. But a questioning of many of the fundamental proposals now began. The new central planning machinery was being established; of particular significance was the fact that the number of local authorities with planning powers was to be decimated, and that individually they would be much more powerful. The idea of a National Parks Commission, and its powers, was reassessed in the light of new administrative developments, both centrally and locally. As we shall see, there were real doubts in the minds of Government Departments about what was intended for National Parks, and these were communicated to Silkin. It took some time for a firm conclusion to be expressed but by at least April 1948 a final view had been reached. The Secretary to the Ministry, Sir Thomas Sheepshanks, wrote for internal consumption: 'The Minister doubts whether there is a real case for a new organisation at all, though he thinks there is a case for some Exchequer Assistance to planning authorities and other organisations in order to secure a high standard of preservation and for the provision of the necessary facilities for, for example, refreshment and accommodation. In view, however, of the general expectations and because there is a need for some Exchequer assistance which can probably be better disbursed by some independent body than a Minister, he thinks that a National Commission should be established with responsibility for areas of natural beauty, i.e. not only the named National Parks but also some at any rate of the Conservation Areas.'[73] This observation suggests that the reluctance to accept the need for legislation was overcome by a realistic appraisal of political expectations.

As to the contents of the legislation, the Minister's early thoughts were in the direction of a general Amenities Bill, including not only the questions of National Parks, footpaths and access, but other matters too. These included minerals and the restoration of mining land; he was attracted to the idea of a financial levy in aid of restoration, but there was uncertainty as to the future of the iron and steel industry, and early legislation was not possible. The Mineral Workings Act, 1951, which set up the Ironstone Restoration Fund, was to deal with this matter later. The question of the preservation of important buildings was also in mind. The Georgian Group was pressing for a power to contribute out of public funds towards the cost of the upkeep of fine historic buildings. In fact, the Gowers Committee on Historic Houses took over this aspect, and subsequent legislation came with the Historic Buildings and Ancient Monuments Act, 1953. The Minister was also concerned about the clearance of shacks but he seemed to be assured that his own Town and Country Planning Act, 1947, gave adequate powers to deal with this matter.

The proposed legislation quickly settled down therefore into three aspects: National Parks, footpaths and access to the countryside. He could be assured of a widespread measure of support from bodies such as the Commons Society, the Youth Hostels Association, the Ramblers Association and the Councils for the Preservation of Rural England and Wales. On the other hand, other country users as represented by the National Farmers Union, the Forestry Commission, the Central Landowners Association and the British Field Sports Society had different interests. But the Minister could be encouraged by other straws in the wind which suggested an encouraging breadth of support. The Gathering Grounds Sub-Committee of the Ministry of Health's Central Advisory Committee was sitting in 1947 and it was known that liberal recommendations were likely as to public access in gathering grounds. In this situation, aided by the Hobhouse and Dower Reports, the Minister became committed to his legislative programme.

The Ministry of Town and Country Planning. The Ministry's officials were beset with early doubts about the need for legislation. They were particularly concerned about the role and function of the proposed Commission. There was no great conviction about the need for National Parks, and there was antipathy towards the idea of a Commission because of the uncertainty about the nature of the job it might do. The Reports of Hobhouse and Ramsay still left many unsettled questions; the runaway enthusiasm for the National Parks proposals and the suggested systems for administration had to be given effective legislative clothing, and this was not going to be easy. An internal note in November 1947[74] put the issue clearly: 'We shall, I think, need at an early date, to examine much more closely what really is the true concept behind National Parks because confusion of thought in regard to the concept is leading to quite exaggerated notions as to what standard is possible, or as to what the machinery should be for securing it.

'The problem of the relationship of a National Parks Commission, if established, to the Department and the Minister is more difficult than hitherto we had realised, and to settle functions for the Commission which would give them a real job to do without conflict and overlap with the proper functions of the Department, will, I suspect, prove to be a difficult task to which we had better address ourselves as soon as possible.'

It was known that the Minister at first saw little real need for a National Parks Commission, but felt that circumstances dictated that there should be one. The officials followed this line, namely that having received the Hobhouse Report, and because of public expectations surrounding it, they were now obliged to set up a National Commission with such functions as they could devise. But there were difficulties in this for the bureaucracy. For example: one of the aims of National Parks was to secure a high standard of planning. But wasn't this standard to be achieved elsewhere? Grant was payable anywhere under s.94 of the Town and Country Planning Act, 1947, for the removal of unsightly development: were higher rates of grant to be payable where a very strong national interest could be claimed? A note from Sheepshanks, the Secretary, to the Minister in April 1948 expressed the officials' concern over the legislation and in particular about the Commission. 'I more than ever have the feeling that the case for legislation is very weak, and that so far as administrative merits are concerned an informed critic could demolish most of our arguments pretty easily.' With regard to the Commission as proposed by Hobhouse, he wrote: 'I feel bound to repeat the warning that I have given you before that this might quite possibly prejudice the future existence of this Department. As you know we are inevitably regarded by many of the older Departments as a fifth wheel in the coach. It might be said that a sixth wheel in the shape of an independent Commission for country or amenity planning would be quite intolerable. The concluding argument might be that amenity or country planning is the one function which justified an independent defender of its own and it would be better that that defender might be the proposed new Commission and that the Ministry of Town and Country Planning might therefore cease to exist.'[75]

Uncertainty, reluctance, and lack of enthusiasm among the officials could not bode well for the imagination that was required for the new legislation. But from May 1948, the Minister having declined to follow his Secretary's warning, the Department was putting together draft items for inclusion in the Bill. That month the Deputy Secretary, Evelyn Sharp, prepared a paper for the

Minister which suggested some general lines of approach. There would be a National Parks Commission with central headquarters and a permanent staff; the Chairman, vice-Chairman and members would be assembled on a part-time basis. As to the role of the Commission, National Parks would be proposed in the first instance by the planning authorities; the Commission would be interested in the plan for the area and also in any important projected development. Cases of disagreement would be referred to the Minister, with the Commission entitled to make representation to planning authorities and other organisations. With regard to powers, high rates of grant would be payable to remove eyesores; there would be extra payment for the removal of overhead electric cables in exceptional cases; there would be compensation (again, exceptionally) for the necessary use of more expensive building materials; and there were to be contributions towards high quality planning staff in the smaller counties.

The Treasury. From the start the Treasury had no enthusiasm for a National Parks Commission.[76] Internal notes indicate that it was thought a Commission as proposed by Hobhouse was unnecessary on the grounds that planning control could be looked after under the planning powers provided by the 1947 Act and that management could be entrusted to a grant-aided body on the lines of the Arts Council. All the executive work could be entrusted to the Park Committees and all supervision to the Minister. It was believed that there was a proliferation of Government landlords of amenity land; already there was the Forestry Commission, the Agricultural Land Commission, Commissioners of Crown Lands, the Central Land Board and the Ministry of Works (for Ancient Monuments). There would be added complications with two National Parks Commissions and the National Trust. Finally, it was considered that the financial arrangements proposed in Hobhouse were muddled. As one Departmental observer put it in November 1947: 'a National Parks Commission would only make work and there is little more case for it than a National New Towns Commission'.

The actual influence of the Treasury began to be felt when Government papers were drawn up, upon which Departmental observations were required. There was regular contact between the Ministry of Town and Country Planning and the Treasury over financial matters, and the attitudes of the Chancellor and the officials during this time of economic stringency became very important. It was made clear to M.T.C.P. that certain desirable provisions were unacceptable. There was a certain amount of 'brinkmanship' in the negotiations and the full weight of Minister, Chancellor and Secretaries was occasionally brought to bear. Pressure by M.T.C.P. to secure the maximum that could be obtained sometimes pushed the Treasury into a hostile reaction, but the new Ministry understandably was under pressure from outside sources to meet the spirit of the countryside lobby.

For some time the financial implications of the proposed Bill were unclear. Indeed, it was thought that they could perhaps not be clarified until a Commission was set up, in which case it would be best to ask for an annual sum of money, asking the Commission to put up each year a scheme for Treasury approval. There were four possibilities for financial arrangements: (a) special vote, (b) grant-in-aid borne on the Minister's vote, (c) grant payable from the Minister's vote, and (d) receipts and payments of the Commission to be included under appropriate sub-heads of the Ministry's vote. The Treasury were inclined to favour the special vote, whereas the Ministry expressed a preference for a grant-in-aid or a grant, as this would bring the expenditure under the general control of the Ministry.

Other early consultations took place on the extent of Exchequer assistance that could be given in particular cases. These included the question as to whether, in the event of a requirement to build in stone rather than brick in certain areas, compensation might be payable. The Treasury view was that there was great difficulty in financially supporting a person in one part of the country and not another. But this matter was resolved as it became clear that the extra cost of developing in appropriate materials could be made a condition of planning consent, without compensation. Other matters proved of more substance and showed the relative strength of the Treasury in inter-departmental conflicts.

For example, in June 1948 the Deputy Secretary, Evelyn Sharp, enquired of Fraser at the Treasury[77] whether it might be possible to transfer to the Commission the then powers of local authorities, grant-aided under s.94 of the Town and Country Planning Act, 1947, in such matters as tree preservation and removing unsightly development. The Treasury view, communicated by Sir Herbert Brittain, was that there was objection to removing local authorities' powers before they had had a chance of exercising them. Moreover, the effect would be that the cost of exercising these powers would fall entirely on the Exchequer. It was not desirable to select for transfer to the Commission certain powers but not others. Moreover, if the Commission were actually to exercise planning functions direct, would it not materially affect their character as an advisory body? The Treasury therefore rejected the suggestion. Evelyn Sharp's answer to this rebuff is interesting because it throws into sharp light the extreme difficulty the Ministry found itself in in relation to the definition of the Commission's role. She confessed that the suggestion had been her own, and was in fact not supported by her Secretary. She had a deep distrust of a grant-aided service. She wrote: 'I cannot help feeling that the Commission is going to be a pretty frustrated body (in much the same way as this Ministry is an extremely frustrated body) if it has to proceed entirely by persuading County Councils instead of taking a little direct action themselves. A form of default power, you know, is not a real answer.'

There was also the question of support for local authorities. It became clear at an early date that the rural counties with small populations were going to have financial and manpower difficulties in meeting their National Park obligations. The Treasury line was strongly expressed at a meeting in June 1948, requested by the Future Legislation Committee, between the Lord President, the Minister, the Secretary and W. S. Murrie.[78] The Treasury indicated that they would object to the Commission having power to spend money when the expenditure could be incurred by local authorities. There was considerable apprehension of future pressure for a very high rate of expenditure by the Commission. The Treasury would have less objection if the forthcoming Bill laid down a fixed annual sum for the Commission's expenditure with power to increase the sum by Order subject to affirmative resolution.

The Treasury also disliked a suggestion of the Minister that the Commission should have power to contribute to the cost of extra staff employed by local authorities for National Park functions. Discussion on this disagreement went on for some months. The Chancellor, Stafford Cripps, later informed the Minister personally that he was very much opposed to contribution being made to the cost of local authority staffs.[79] Subsequently the Chancellor offered another suggestion, that the Commission might second staff to local authorities from time to time to assist them in their functions. But Silkin wrote to Cripps in November asking for a reconsideration of his view about grants payable to planning authorities for the cost of staff in National Park areas, explaining that the County Councils Association were hostile to the idea of staff seconded from the Commission. Cripps replied in December to the effect that he still could not agree to Silkin's request. He pointed out that the poorer an authority was, the more the Exchequer now shared in costs through the Equalisation Grant, and in any case, there were objections in principle. He observed: 'I should be very sorry to agree that unimaginative or supine administration of National Parks, Town and Country Planning, Housing or anything else justified an Exchequer grant as an inducement to the authority to take on the staff necessary for the efficient discharge of its duties! I cannot (therefore) accept either unwillingness or poverty on the part of local authorities as a reason for agreeing to a grant towards administrative expenses, which I regard as wholly undesirable in principle and in no way specially justified in this particular case.

'(Finally) it seems to me that your letter casts grave doubt on the rightness of the admittedly controversial decision to entrust planning and other functions in the National Parks to local authorities instead of to a special body or bodies financed from the Exchequer. As you know, I entirely support your views on that point, but to say that the local authorities are unable or unwilling to administer properly the task assigned to them is to say that your critics are right.'[80] That was the end of the matter. As an episode it illustrated not only the importance of Treasury weight of opinion, but also the uncertainty that still existed about the future of National Parks administration.

At the June meeting Treasury views also made it clear that it was desirable to limit Exchequer assistance in a geographical sense. The concern of the Commission should be limited to National Park areas, at least in the first stage. It was no doubt remembered that Hobhouse's 12 National Parks and 52 Conservation Areas totalled 27% of the area of the country. It was as important not to dissipate energies as it was not to scatter the financial resources too thinly.

With regard to the role of the Commission the Treasury's attitude constantly implied constraint. The Treasury was doubtful of the Commission's powers and responsibilities outside National Parks. They did not like the idea of the Commission contributing the whole cost of some operations. They did not want the Commission to have any power to acquire and hold land. They were against the proposition that the Commission should have reserve power to provide hotel and catering accommodation; instead, grants should be made through existing organisations. They thought that no money should be payable to encourage the placing of cables underground: it was argued that this was something the planning authorities could require when new cables were proposed, without paying compensation. It was agreed that financial support could be given for such as parking spaces, camping sites, laybys and viewpoints, but not for museums and institutes.

The Commission. As we have seen, the role, function and powers of the proposed Commission were the subject of considerable debate during this phase, and pressure continued to be exerted during 1949 one way and another by the various interest groups. Although it was soon acceded that a Commission would have to be established, there were fundamental difficulties to overcome. Perhaps (with hindsight) they were insuperable, reflecting as they did unavoidable conflicts, stemming from the sharing of responsibilities and the exercise of powers by two bodies, Government and Commission.

From the start, there was the question of what planning powers should be entrusted to the Commission. The Minister's early inclination was not to entrust any central development body with any planning functions other than the giving of advice. He therefore suggested that planning powers should be left with the County Councils. The Lord President in March 1948 however thought the right course was to entrust planning powers to the Commission.[81]

At the heart of the matter there was the conflict of function between the Ministry and the proposed new body. The functions suggested by Hobhouse for the Commission included the giving of advice, the disbursement of monies, education of the public, acquisition of land and the carrying out of development supplemental to existing authorities and organisations. The last two were quickly curtailed and it became obvious that if the Commission's duties were limited to the remainder then the point might be taken that a Commission with powers so limited was a farce. This might result in a claim that the Commission should be consulted and have an opportunity of making representations not only before any development plan was submitted to the Minister but before any development took place for which other Ministers were responsible. Even the very function of advice-giving was suspect. Potential conflict between the Commission and the Department was apparent: after all, who held the skills? These questions led Sheepshanks to make some suggestions to the Minister in April 1948 as to the possible functions and status of the Commission.[82] A constraining hand was well in evidence. He thought that the function of the Commission should be prescribed by regulations so that adaptations could be made in the light of experience. On finance he suggested that the Commission should put up a scheme showing what they proposed to spend and on what general purposes. With regard to their supervisory duties he recommended that the Commission should not receive development plans, but rather observe upon them, believing that the extra consultation would be quite intolerable. (A related point of great concern to the Department was whether the Commission should appear as an independent witness at enquiries. Although there would be advantage in publicly cross-examining an amenity view, none the less it would be embarrassing for the Commission to state their view in public when the Minister ultimately had to reach a decision.)

The months of 1948 went by with constant confusion and indeed anxiety about the sort of Commission that was being created. The usual view was that the Commission should have jurisdiction only in the National Park areas. But in May 1948 there was a suggestion for a rather different form of Commission. A note from Evelyn Sharp to the Minister read, 'What we now think is that the better solution might be to compromise by setting up what you might call a "Commission for Rural England" with special responsibilities in areas defined as National Parks.'[83] Nothing came of this, but twenty years later the establishment of the Countryside Commission expressed the same point.

Uncertainty over the Commission's powers and duties was eased when agreement was reached in June 1948 between the Minister and the Chancellor that the Commission was to be advisory and not an operating body. The implications of this were to cause difficulties later, and there was still uneasiness about the situation. An apt internal Departmental note in August made comparison with other Commissions: if the National Parks Commission was to be advisory why was it necessary to make statutory provision about it? The Royal Fine Art Commission was advisory but was not set up by statute. It was too late for fundamental rethinking of this kind, but suspicion about the proposed Commission continued. Another internal note in November read: 'Everything turns, of course, on what sort of Commission you get, but if the Commission had to be packed with enthusiasts of the "Hands off National Parks" type, embarrassment would be too mild a word. . . . I think the fact is that once we let in the Commission on planning matters at all there is no escape from the risk of conflicting advice.'[84]

To make matters worse, it was not even possible for the Minister to have absolute control over the appointment of a Secretary to the Commission. In view of what happened over s.2 of the Town and Country Planning Bill in Committee the Minister realised he could not retain the power of appointment in his own hands. (An amendment to the Bill, proposing that the Central Land Board and not the Minister should appoint the Secretary, was defeated. But in the Lords Committee the amendment that the Board should appoint the Secretary with the approval of the Minister was moved and accepted without discussion.)

Standing Committee (C.P.R.E. and W.). After the publication of the Hobhouse Report in May 1947 the Standing Committee on National Parks of the Councils for the Preservation of Rural England and Wales submitted observations to the Minister in September in the form of a 14-page memorandum.

This was a document designed to ensure the highest possible status for the Commission. For example, whereas the Hobhouse Report expressly stated (para. 91) that the Commission should not take over the functions of the Minister as the central planning authority, the Standing Committee wished to see the powers of the Commission enhanced to a point at which they would be comparable with those enjoyed by the Forestry Commissioners, *vis à vis* the Minister of Agriculture. Many of the subsequent recommendations stemmed from this first assumption. For example, it was urged that the Commission should be charged by statute with a duty to initiate and define planning policy for National Parks. Additionally, it was argued that the Commission should review all development projects affecting National Parks before such projects were approved by the Minister. Furthermore, the Commission should have power to 'call in' cases of conflict between local and national interests to decide itself. There was insistence that the Minister should always deal with the Commission and never directly with a Park committee. On the other hand, the Chairman of the Commission should enjoy direct access, without using the Minister as an intermediary, to Government Departments, Chairmen of Public Corporations and the Chairman of the Central Land Board on all development projects affecting National Parks. Moreover, the Commission should be empowered to participate, as a third adjudicator, at Joint Ministerial hearings of appeals by statutory undertakings against decisions of local planning authorities, or at the hearing of cases called in by the Minister; the Commission should also be empowered to participate as an adjudicator at public local enquiries. The Standing Committee urged a formal procedure of appeal instituted by statute for use in cases where agreement could not be reached. It was suggested that there might be an appeal to a permanent Committee of the Cabinet or of Ministers, or to a Committee of the Privy Council, or to a Standing Committee of both Houses. It was also argued that the Commission should be empowered to appear before Private Bill Committees; and that the Commission should have the status of a petitioner and a right to be heard by the Joint Committee of both Houses under special Parliamentary procedure.

With regard to organisation at the local level, the Standing Committee continued to express their great fear of the undue strength of local interests. They recommended, as a safeguard for national interests, that two-thirds of the members of park committees should be nominated instead of half as Hobhouse had decided. They also urged that the Commission should be empowered to nominate one of its own members to be chairman of every park committee and to appoint the planning officer.

The memorandum was carefully analysed by Sir Philip Magnus in a Departmental note.[85] He concluded that 'the general intention of the C.P.R.E. is sound, but that the helpfulness of some of the detailed points which they make is impaired by the fact that the Minister of Town and Country Planning himself has no such authority, except over private individuals and local councils, as that which the C.P.R.E. appears to postulate on behalf of the National Parks Commission'. The Standing Committee's object of securing an enhanced status for the Commission inevitably raised the question of the future relationship between the Commission and the Minister. As Magnus observed, 'it is inconceivable that the Minister of Town and Country Planning should be content to allow the National Parks Commission to ignore his authority!' The whole question of roles, function and powers was implied, and was not to be easily resolved.

The Minister with the Permanent Secretary, Parliamentary Secretary and Departmental officials met a deputation from the Standing Committee in December 1947. The meeting provided the opportunity for a clear statement on preliminary positions. The Minister indicated that he had not yet made up his mind about machinery for implementing National Parks. He said that having just created new and larger planning authorities under the Town and Country Planning Act, 1947, he would be reluctant to take planning powers away from them before they had a chance to show what they could do. To make the National Parks Commission analogous to the Forestry Commission in dealing with areas as a whole would mean telling 20 out of 63 county councils that they could not be trusted to do the job and their powers must be handed over to a non-elected body.

For their part, the Standing Committee wished to ensure that National Parks were a national rather than local authority concern, protected and administered on a higher standard than the rest of the country. They therefore visualised very much wider powers for the Commission than the Hobhouse Committee had contemplated. To this, the Minister replied that he visualised the job of the Commission as an advisory one and that the 1947 Act would adequately safeguard National Park areas through the new local planning authorities which would come into existence on the appointed day in July 1948.

Lord Birkett, as Chairman of the Standing Committee, did not attend this meeting because of his absence on the Northern Circuit at the time. However in his capacity he made a belated intervention to the Minister in a letter of 18 January 1948. The minutes of the December meeting had been greeted with 'alarm and despondency', and Birkett had been asked to write and express the sense of frustration which the interview had given. The Minister was seemingly intending to rely on the new large planning authorities without any form of compulsory combination into Joint Boards. Additionally, the Minister was rejecting the idea of a strong Commission with national interests and with direct responsibility for a common policy and high standards. Birkett's letter spoke of 'great disappointment'. He recollected that 'Ten years ago we interviewed the Minister of Health. We were told to go away and educate public opinion. In this we have had some success. And those, who, since then, have formed the idea of a new and special planning category for National Parks, and have come to value it and work for it hopefully, will feel it as a blow to the usefulness and power of the Ministry of Town and

Country Planning that it had now decided to let this opportunity go by, in which it could have played an open and emphatic part in building up a national system of National Parks. For not only did you reject our proposals for giving, as we think, true effect to the underlying intention, in matters of planning, of the Hobhouse Report: you also rejected the proposals, in these matters, of the Hobhouse Report itself.'[86]

Birkett was a respected figure of great influence, and his place in the history of National Parks is no mean one. Silkin had dinner with him on 5 February, and contact was maintained through a further letter from Birkett later that month. It was a reminder to the Minister that two major matters were at the heart of the proposed legislation: the character and powers of the Commission, and the constitution of the Park Committee. Birkett wrote: 'The first duty of the National Parks Commission is in planning (protection) not in "management". It should have the right to review the decisions of the Park Committee if they should offend against the national standards laid down by the Commission; and in the case of other Departments of Government—which by law can and will override the local planning committee—the Commission should have the clear right to refer the questions of conflict to some recognised tribunal of appeal.'[87] As far as the Park Committees were concerned, the national interest should be fully represented.

The Standing Conference maintained their pressure, and on 15 March H. G. Griffin, Secretary of the C.P.R.E., sent a note to the Minister about the planning situation that would arise in the Lake District and in the Peak on 1 July when the 1947 Act became operative. They were keen to suggest that there could be no reliance placed on the new units of administration that the 1947 Act would create. In the Lake District the situation was that in Westmorland the County Architect would become the County Planning Officer. In Cumberland the County Surveyor was Planning Officer. In Lancashire there was to be a County Planning Department, but the Lancashire Lake District would be in the charge of two planning assistants and a draughtsman. In the regional divisions of the Ministry Cumberland and Westmorland came under one regional controller, and Lancashire another. The Joint Advisory Planning Committee for the Lake District would have no Planning Officer and no executive power; it was a weak and indeterminate body which had not met since July 1947. (The first Joint Committee, born in 1935, died after 18 months.)

With regard to the Peak District, it was expected that planning would proceed as part of the administration of minor and unrelated parts of five different planning authorities. In Cheshire the Peak area covered 4% of the total area of the planning authority, in

Derbyshire it was 35%, Sheffield 15%, Staffordshire 7% and the West Riding 3%. The Peak Joint Planning Committee in Derbyshire covered more than 60% of the proposed National Park: this needed to be extended to the remainder.

The Minister was impressed by these arguments[88] and thought that the Lord President's paper, then in preparation (see page 96) should set out the arguments both for and against the Hobhouse recommendations. Preference so far had been in favour of departure from those recommendations, but there should be no final commitment to this view; the influence of the Standing Committee had made its mark, even if it was not to win the day.

County Councils Association. By comparison, the influence of the County Councils Association was less marked. An informal meeting was held on 9 March 1948[89] between Sheepshanks, with departmental officials, and Sir Arthur Hobhouse, accompanied by four other representatives of the Association. The Secretary explained that it appeared objectionable in principle that planning in National Park areas should be entrusted to any other body than the local planning authorities. A distinction was possible between planning and development functions, and therefore it seemed possible to set up machinery for the development of National Parks without interfering with the new local planning administrative structure. Therefore, the Minister was at present disposed to favour the idea of a central Commission charged with development functions but without planning jurisdiction. On the other hand Hobhouse's deputation felt it wrong to disassociate planning from development. Furthermore, the Ministry's role was one primarily concerned with control of land use, not of amenity: that was for another body. There was a view too that county councils might feel embarrassed about assuming development functions in National Park areas, on the grounds that 'management' was not really within the purview of local authorities.

The confrontation was later described by Sheepshanks as a 'very unsatisfactory meeting with what purported to be representatives of the County Councils' Association but appeared to be little more than Sir Arthur Hobhouse's claque'.[90] None the less it suggested that some attention should be given to the alleged difficulties of separating planning and management and the suggested duplication of staff by Ministry and Commission. In a subsequent letter to Hobhouse on 15 March, Sheepshanks confirmed that 'the only issue of principle where there was difficulty was the proposal that the planning authority for the park areas should not be County Councils or Joint Boards of County Councils but an *ad hoc* body consisting as to half of nominees of the Parks Commission and as to half of representatives nominated by the Local Authorities'.[91]

The value of the C.C.A.'s observations was somewhat weakened by two factors. In the first place Hobhouse's own position had been known to change. He had originally regarded it as a matter of fundamental importance that there should be separate bodies in each Park for both planning and management functions. John Dower had advocated a single body and his view ultimately prevailed. It was thought now that Hobhouse's insistence on the inseparability of planning and development functions was based more on adherence to the compromise view reached in his Committee than any basis of principle. Secondly, it became clear that the C.C.A. itself was divided about the Hobhouse recommendations. The Planning Committee of the Association took the view that planning should be in the hands of the local authorities.[92]

The question of planning at the local level in National Parks was a thorny one. There were two early schools of thought about the Hobhouse recommendations. Firstly, it was possible to have a National Parks Commission responsible for the job in all Park areas, without any local Park committees; this idea was rejected at an early stage. Secondly, it was possible to entrust the task to a local body working under the supervision of the Ministry, without any central Commission, such as on the lines of the New Towns; this too was rejected.

Some kind of local machine was necessary, however, and there seemed to be two options. First there might be reliance entirely on the new local government units, on the grounds that local Park committees, as suggested by Hobhouse, were unnecessary because the county councils could do everything required in the way of supervision. Second, there might be Park committees of joint composition, in which case the issue was one of proportional representation between local authority and Minister-nominated members.

An internal Departmental view towards the middle of 1948[93] was that with planning powers transferred to County Councils there was no object in setting up Park Committees. Some of Hobhouse's Conservation Areas were as important to the public as some of the National Parks, and as the chief distinction that Hobhouse made between the two was that Parks were to have Committees while Conservation Areas need not, then this slender difference encouraged criticism of the whole Park Committee concept. But the strength of the view that National Parks were national and not simply of local significance led to the Park Committee idea being accepted. (The Lord President's Committee in July 1948 which considered a memorandum from the Minister is crucial in this respect. See page 97.) From then onwards the concern was about composition of the Committees.

Phase Two, from mid-1948

The Lord President's Committee considered a preliminary paper on the proposed Amenities Bill in April 1948.[94] This came at a time when there was still uncertainty about the function of the proposed Commission in relation to the Ministry of Town and Country Planning and when the Standing Conference and the C.C.A. were maintaining their own pressures. Inevitably, the paper left many loose ends and the Treasury also made known their reservations on financial matters. A comment on this meeting by the Deputy Secretary was that 'the result was a very brief discussion at which in effect it was said that our proposals were still half baked (as is true) and that there were a number of consultations we ought to have with other Departments'.[95]

Silkin's Memorandum for the Lord President's Committee was entitled 'National Parks, Footpaths and Access to Uncultivated Land, and Wild Life Conservation'. It recapitulated the recommendations of the Hobhouse Report and acknowledged the general expectation that existed concerning the provision of new machinery for the establishment and running of National Parks. But while 'close and sympathetic consideration' to the proposals had been given, the Minister 'did not feel convinced that the somewhat elaborate machinery proposed' was necessary. He observed that 'About the Hobhouse proposals there hangs a general implication that neither the local planning authorities nor, indeed, the Minister of Planning himself can be trusted to show a proper appreciation of the value of preserving national parks and other areas of high scenic value'.

Silkin thought, however, that 'there are sound arguments for some kind of national commission to assist and advise on securing, directly or indirectly, a high standard of amenity and improved access and accommodation in the parks and also in the conservation areas'. He was satisfied that there was a good case for providing Exchequer assistance to planning authorities and other organisations to enable these objectives to be secured, and he thought it more satisfactory for this Exchequer assistance to be disbursed by a semi-independent body such as a Commission rather than by a Minister. He proceeded to frame the Commission's draft terms of reference: essentially advisory, but also to disburse monies and to exercise reserve powers. With regard to local administration, the Minister, in discussion, dismissed the idea of local Park committees exercising the same powers as those exercised by local planning authorities under the 1947 Act.

The Minister's paper also dealt with access to countryside. He generally accepted the proposals made in the Report of the Special Committee on Footpaths and Access (Cmd. 7207), though with reservations about compensation for damage and about the assignment to Quarter Sessions of *all* the questions relating to rights of way. He thought that diversions of an existing right of way or the creation of a new one should be a Departmental matter and not for a Court of Law, but in discussion, the Home Secretary, Chuter Ede, was of the opinion that both kinds of dispute should be dealt with by Quarter Sessions.

Silkin asked for authorisation to prepare a Bill to establish a Commission to carry out the functions suggested and to provide for improved access to the countryside. It would also be necessary to supplement the powers of the 1947 Act to give protection to wild life and to conserve nature. (The establishment of a Biological Service, proposed by the Wild Life Conservation Special Committee, was already being considered by the Lord President.) There were clearly a number of outstanding issues in the Minister's Memorandum which remained for discussion with the Departments concerned, and the Minister was asked to circulate a further Memorandum.

This was submitted to the Lord President's Committee in July 1948, entitled 'National Parks, Footpaths and Access to Uncultivated Land'.[96] The paper considered a number of points which had not been fully clarified at the previous meeting. The Minister still proposed to leave the administration of National Parks to County Councils as the planning authorities. When a Council failed to carry out 'desirable National Park development', the Minister proposed to rely on his power of 'call in' and also act in default of a planning authority if necessary. The Bill would oblige local planning authorities to consult the Commission on proposed development within a National Park. In discussion, the Minister said that he was satisfied that to establish Park committees of the Hobhouse kind would lead to administrative confusion. This was agreed but it was felt that the Bill should provide that the local authority(ies) concerned should set up a special committee responsible for the National Park area. It was accepted that in all but two of the National Parks proposed by Hobhouse more than one local planning authority was concerned; in five there were three or more authorities. The Minister stated that he would need to be satisfied in these cases about the machinery proposed for joint handling of the area.

The Minister had amended some of his earlier proposals, as a result of discussion. With regard to National Park areas, in his earlier Memorandum he thought that the responsibilities of the Commission should extend to most, if not all of the Conservation Areas, proposed in the Hobhouse Report, in addition to the twelve National Parks. He now proposed that the areas to be defined as National Parks should be limited to extensive areas of beautiful and relatively wild country, and that outside these areas the Commission would simply have certain limited functions for the protection and enhancement of any area of outstanding natural beauty (perhaps 12–15 all told). Within the Park areas the Commission would be entitled to be consulted by the planning authority on their planning proposals. In addition to this 'watch dog' function the Commission would be empowered to finance or contribute to various special purposes in the Parks. With regard to acquisition of land, the Commission would not hold land itself, but would enable acquisition by the National Trust or a County Council.

The Minister hoped to be able to assist in the provision of hotel and catering accommodation, through liaison with the British Tourist and Holidays Board. He would not wish to rule out the possibility of subsidising accommodation, but this was a point for further discussion with the Treasury. The Chancellor of the Exchequer, Stafford Cripps, had intimated that he would consider sympathetically proposals for making available for the development of National Parks some of the money in the National Land Fund.

In his earlier Memorandum the Minister thought that the settlement of a dispute about an existing right of way should be dealt with by his Department. However, to accommodate the views of the Home Secretary, he now agreed that these disputes should be referred to Quarter Sessions, subject to the simplification of procedure. The Hobhouse Committee had proposed that local planning authorities should be obliged to map all existing rights of way within a period of four years; the Minister now would substitute a power for a duty. With regard to long distance rights of way, it was now proposed that the Commission should be responsible for their creation and maintenance.

As to access to uncultivated land, the Minister proposed to enable planning authorities to declare a public right of access to specified areas of uncultivated land in National Parks and to specified areas of beach and foreshore (within or without National Parks), where there was reason to suppose that conferment of the right would be a public advantage; compensation would be payable. The proposal did not go very much further than the provisions of the Access to Mountains Act, 1939, but important differences were that it put the responsibility primarily on the planning authorities instead of an interested party and it provided for compensation. This was not enough for the Chancellor of the Duchy of Lancaster, Hugh Dalton, who thought the proposed provisions regarding access to uncultivated land should be strengthened. In particular he felt there should be unrestricted access to the beach and foreshore except where it could be shown that there was good reason for excluding the public.

There were two other far-reaching suggestions made in discussion; one was blocked and another came to nothing. First the Minister of Defence, Viscount Alexander, suggested that the Minister might consider the exclusion from the purview of local planning authorities of all land held by Service Departments. The general view of the Committee was that this would not be possible. Second, the importance of encouraging the creation of green belt areas was emphasised. The Minister undertook to consider whether any provision should be included in the Bill for securing an adequate contribution towards the cost of such areas from the local authorities of the adjoining built up areas, but the idea was allowed to be lost at this time.

General approval, subject to outstanding points, was given to the Minister to proceed with the preparation of the Bill. The Future Legislation Committee had provisionally accepted the Bill for the next session, and it was now possible to make progress. There were still uncertainties, and changing ideas over titles indicated these. The Lord President thought the 'Amenities Bill' not a very inspiring title; the Minister himself thought it possible to improve on 'National Parks and Amenities'. Further inspiration came from the Deputy Secretary who suggested 'Commission for the Care of the Countryside'. The Minister thought this 'a little alliterative', preferring 'Commission for the Countryside'. It was not until January 1949 that he indicated a wish for the Bill to be called 'National Parks and Access to the Countryside'.

After the Lord President's Committee in July, the next nine months were spent in preparing the draft legislation and considering the comments of the Departments concerned. There were a number of immediate issues that required further consideration. For example: the Minister was of the opinion that the Bill must leave the National Park areas to be defined later because their boundaries had not been surveyed. In the event, there was no great resistance to this, but the precedent of the Development Areas defined in the Distribution of Industry Act, 1945, was against him in this respect. Second, the size of the Commission was not yet settled; there were also the questions of the people to be appointed and the staff to be engaged. Next, there was the thorny problem of land acquisition in National Parks. Hobhouse had contemplated extensive acquisitions, and the Chancellor of the Duchy of Lancaster might urge this from the National Land Fund. But it had to be remembered that while before the war virtually the only way of preserving beautiful country was through public ownership, planning control through the 1947 Act could achieve this. Lastly, agreement with the Treasury had still to be obtained on a number of issues. For example, financial assistance in areas of outstanding natural beauty was likely to be requested. But there was a danger of slipping into a position where the normal planning grant, not yet ruled out, was regarded as insufficient in many cases for which it was designed.

In September, instructions were given to Parliamentary Counsel for preparation of the Bill. In October, reference was made to forthcoming legislation in the King's Speech. Copies of the first print of the Bill were circulated in December to relevant Departments for comment. In February 1949 the Minister submitted a Memorandum to the Lord President's Committee entitled 'National Parks and Access to the Countryside',[97] in which he outlined the main provisions of the Bill before a final draft was prepared for the Legislation Committee.

He drew his colleagues' attention to a number of points. The staffing of the Commission had been the subject of a disagreement between the Minister and the Treasury. The point at issue arose on the question as to whether or not the Commission should be a Department of Government, the practical issue being whether their staff should be civil servants or not. The Minister attached importance to underlining the independence of the Commission by giving them a certain freedom in the recruitment and pay of their staff. The Treasury took the view that it would be preferable for the Commission's staff to be civil servants. A few days before the meeting of the Lord President's Committee, Sir Bernard Gilbert had written to Sir Thomas Sheepshanks, the Departmental Secretary, that 'it would be quite wrong that the staff of the Commission should be anything but Civil Servants. . . . Your proposal is merely reviving the long discontinued and thoroughly discredited policy of lump sum employment for those engaged in the activities of Government.'[98] The Committee found in favour of the Treasury on this matter, and Silkin's proposal was lost.

With regard to the question of payment for Chairman and Vice Chairman of the Commission the Minister had discussed this with the Lord President, H. Morrison, and they agreed that these two persons should be paid. The Lord President was doubtful about the payment of members; the Minister thought it would be unfortunate not to take power to pay all the members, although this might prove unnecessary. He found it impossible to say how much work would fall to the Commission, because the allocation of functions between members of the Commission and their officers was not yet known. The Committee decided that the Bill should provide for payment to the Chairman and Vice Chairman only.

The Minister's Memorandum stated that the Bill would provide that local planning authorities must set up special Park committees, and, where necessary, Joint Boards or joint advisory committees for Park administration. With regard to the composition of these committees or boards, the Lord President and the Minister were recommending three members, or such greater number as the Minister might determine, not exceeding 25% of the whole, to be nominated by the Minister after consultation with the Commission.

The difficulty about a flat 25% nomination, as previously agreed, was that this might mean having to find a very large number of persons if the committee happened to be a large one. The Minister advised the Committee of the opposition of the County Councils and Municipal Corporations to this arrangement. However, he thought they would agree to a provision which required them to co-opt not less than three members, capable of representing the national interest, in agreement with the Minister or Commission. The Minister sought advice as to whether there should be an escape clause providing that the Minister could agree to nomination of less than three members if necessary (for example, the difficulty of finding people in small areas).

This met with the opposition of Dalton, Chancellor of the Duchy of Lancaster; he too submitted a Memorandum to the Lord President's Committee.[99] He argued the case of national versus local authority parks. He described many of the local authorities concerned as 'politically reactionary': they would be apt to take a local view, to pay undue regard to increased rateable value, and to the vested interests of private landowners. In the Peak National Park, for example, much of the land was owned by the Dukes and others who had ruled to exclude the public from reasonable access. He argued that there should be adherence to the principle decided upon at the Lord President's Committee in July 1948, and suggested a 'formula of conciliation': that the Minister should in all cases appoint 25% of the members, after consultation, both with the National Parks Commission and with the local authorities concerned. The Committee finally agreed to this viewpoint, and Silkin's attempt to pacify local authority objection was overruled.

The Minister outlined the range of powers which he proposed to give to Park planning authorities. There would be powers to acquire land: all authorities would have power to purchase land by agreement, and to purchase land compulsorily for the restoration of derelict land, the planting of trees, the provision of accommodation, parking places, camping places, camping sites, and facilities for sport; also land to which access could be given by Order. The Chancellor of the Duchy of Lancaster in his Memorandum wanted powers of acquisition to be 'simple and strong'. He hoped that in a few years' time most of the land in most of the Parks would be either publicly-owned or owned by some public-spirited, non-profit making body. He wanted the Minister himself to have power to compulsorily acquire land in default of action by local authorities; 'we shall have no peace round the Peak until we have paid off the Dukes', Dalton declared. But the Minister's measures were considered adequate.

The Hobhouse Committee had recommended National Park

Centres in National Parks where local information for the public would be available. The Minister had hoped that these would be provided by the Park planning authorities with grant from the Exchequer, but there was Treasury objection to this, and the Minister was not disposed to press the point.

The Minister's Memorandum referred to the warden service as recommended by Hobhouse. He explained that his Bill would empower Park planning authorities to make byelaws to safeguard the interests of farmers and to prevent the scattering of litter and indiscriminate camping, but contained no provision for a warden service. He did not like the idea of any large body of wardens and preferred to rely on the education of the public in standards of behaviour through the efforts of the Commission. If the occasional warden were needed then 'it should not be too much for the authorities to meet the cost'.

On the question of grants, the Minister's Memorandum indicated that there were a number of matters still to discuss with the Treasury. For example, there was the question of payment of grant for acquisition of access land as distinct from grant towards compensation on the making of an Order, and the possibility of grant higher than 75% towards the cost of remaking or altering unsightly buildings or development. The Bill as then drafted contained a clause under which the Minister might finance acquisition of land by the National Trust, the intention being to make available for the development of the Parks some of the money in the National Land Fund. This was supported by the Chancellor of the Duchy of Lancaster who described the Fund as 'one of my offspring which is at present in a very healthy condition and putting on weight through accumulation of unspent interest'. But the Treasury now wished this clause to be omitted as they were reviewing the whole question of the use of the Fund and the future of the National Trust. The Committee agreed, however, that discussions should continue between the Treasury and the Ministry on this point, the hope being expressed that the Chancellor of the Exchequer would be able to find some way of meeting the Minister's wishes.

Before the Minister's proposals could go to the Legislation Committee in March 1949, there were a number of points to be resolved. These largely concerned the Treasury, and some last minute efforts were made to secure money for the Commission in order to enhance its status. Some of the matters were quite minor, but the Ministry was anxious to press for them, bearing in mind the delicate political position in which the Commission was likely to be placed.

For example, there was the question of expenditure on publicity. The Treasury came to the view that this should not be met by the

Commission but by the Central Office of Information and the Stationery Office.[100] The general policy had recently been under consideration by the Lord President and the Chancellor and the decision to centralise in the C.O.I. had been confirmed. This did not mean that the C.O.I. would necessarily handle all the jobs, but they would bear the cost. This aroused sensitivities about the precise function of the Commission and Sheepshanks felt obliged to complain to Gilbert that virtually the one executive function left to the Commission was now eroded. 'It has always been a cardinal point with us that, in this at least, the Commission should act on their own responsibility, subject to our control of their expenditure,' he wrote.[101] The Minister was concerned about the extremely limited nature of the Commission's executive powers, and there was the likelihood that amendments to strengthen the Commission would have to be accepted during the passage of the Bill. 'The great criticism we are undoubtedly going to meet when the Bill is published is that the Commission will not be in a position to achieve anything of its own motion; and although this matter of the information service is a small thing at least it is something.' Gilbert replied that as to the paucity of the Commission's executive powers, it was fundamental to the agreement reached between the Chancellor and the Minister in June 1948 that the Commission was to be an advisory body and not an operating one. The Treasury could not agree to a clause giving the Commission power themselves to incur expenditure on publicity as a charge to the Minister's Vote.

But in fact the matter did not end there. At the Legislation Committee on 15 March 1949[102] the general feeling was that the procedure whereby the Commission should give information to the Minister and that he should arrange for the C.O.I. to organise the necessary publicity was unnecessarily tortuous. It was more satisfactory to place a direct obligation on the Commission to make information available to users of the Parks. There was no reason to fear that the Commission would engage in too lavish publicity work, and, in any event, their budget would be controlled by the Ministry of Town and Country Planning.

Another example of how the Ministry and the Treasury had to resolve proposals for expenditure occurred over the question of long-distance footpaths. A clause in the draft Bill empowered the Minister to defray expenditure incurred by local planning authorities on these footpaths. The words 'with the consent of the Treasury' had been deleted but the Treasury requested the restoration of the words on the grounds that they were a common form of expression and that Treasury control was provided for in all other spending clauses of the Bill. Dame Evelyn Sharp took up the matter with Sir Herbert

Brittain. An internal Treasury note commented on her pressure:[103]
'This is sheer pique on the part of Dame Evelyn and the Minister who
are always intolerant of Treasury control in any shape or form. . . .
A great deal of time and trouble has been wasted on this Bill through
constant appeals to high authority on trivial points. The Ministry—
some of them—cannot bring themselves to believe that the Treasury
is capable of forming its final view at divisional level. I didn't
have half this trouble on the much more numerous, difficult and
important points thrown up by the Town and Country Planning Act
of 1947.' Brittain replied that the Treasury's request must stand.

One should not make too much of these differences of view. A
raw nerve had been exposed, but the Ministry were being forced to
go to extreme lengths in order to give substance to a form of Commission which would have very few executive powers. At the same
time, there was good reason for Treasury caution on expenditure,
especially on this last item: the Chancellor's agreement to 100%
grant on long-distance paths was on the understanding that there
would be only two or three of them—a total in fact exceeded ultimately. It is difficult, however, for the Historian to assess reliably
the nature of the relationship between the two Departments. But
the suspicion is that the Treasury never saw the National Parks Bill
as a major priority and were not fully sympathetic to the difficulties
in which the Ministry no doubt found itself when trying to meet the
hopes and demands of the lobbyists. An example, in respect of civil
service staff estimates, illustrates this. The actual staff of the Ministry
at the end of January 1949 was 1,106. The Treasury agreed with
the M.T.C.P. Establishments Office to a ceiling of 1,300 during
the next 12 months. Subsequently, the Secretary asked for the
ceiling to be raised to 1,400 in August and 1,500 in February, one
of the considerations being the effect of the National Parks Bill on
manpower estimates. The Treasury response was that if it was a
priority to reduce manpower then the Bill should be postponed.

There remained the question of the role of the National Trust.
The Minister regarded it as essential that the Bill should include a
provision enabling the Exchequer to finance the acquisition and
maintenance of land in a National Park by the National Trust. (It
was thought that the Ministry of Works might exercise compulsory
powers where the National Trust was to hold land, and that the
Minister of Agriculture should acquire agricultural land, subsequently to be handed over to the Agricultural Land Commission
or the Forestry Commission.) But the Treasury objected to the
National Trust proposal, the view being that the Trust was not
suitable in its present form to be, in effect, subsidised by the Government.[104] Additionally, nothing should prejudice a decision on Sir
Ernest Gowers' Committee on Stately Homes.

Having successfully passed the Legislation Committee in March, the Bill could proceed. In introducing his Bill at the second reading (31 March), the Minister claimed that 'This long awaited Bill will be received with great pleasure by a large number of people all over the country who have witnessed with considerable concern disturbing trends in the development of these islands'. These were, firstly, the disfigurement of the countryside, and, secondly, the loss of agricultural land, and its contribution through its pattern of cultivation to the unique character and beauty of the landscape. Thirdly, there was the great lack of public facilities for open-air recreation and for opportunities of access to the countryside. His Bill therefore was directed to arresting and reversing these trends. Its objects were 'first, to preserve and enhance the beauty of the countryside; and secondly, to enable our people to see it, get to it, and enjoy it'.[105] He concluded: 'This is not just a Bill. It is a people's charter—a people's charter for the open air, for the hikers and the ramblers, for everyone who likes to get out into the open air and enjoy the countryside. Without it they are fettered, deprived of their powers of access and facilities needed to make holidays enjoyable. With it the countryside is theirs to preserve, to cherish, to enjoy and to make their own.'[106] This was a politician's flourish, for he knew he could rely on widespread support, but Silkin deserved the praise that came his way.

There were few amendments of any substance to the Bill as it passed through Parliament. These are a matter of public record, and unnecessary to detail in this History. But during this time the Minister and the Department were under private pressure to give assurances in respect of certain interests. For example Silkin was pressed on assurances about Park Planning Committees and the proportion of nominated members. The Minister was reminded of local situations: in the Peak District Mr. Hugh Molson feared financial implications. Molson wrote to Silkin: 'Costs in connection with National Parks are not necessarily popular with the County Councils. To be quite frank with you, the Conservative leader of the Derbyshire County Council is even more hostile to the idea of a National Park than Alderman Charles White, the Labour leader. There is real danger that they will attempt to impose upon my barren and poverty-stricken High Peak the expenditure involved in making it into a National Park.'[107]

Concessions to local sentiment were pressed upon the Minister. For example, Welsh members suggested that the Bill should provide for a Welsh Advisory Committee to which the Commission might refer matters, but this was not accepted. The role of the Commission came under renewed scrutiny and the Minister was asked for an assurance that the Commission would have power under the Bill to issue statements at any time (quite apart from Annual Reports) if it was necessary to do so for the proper exercise of their functions. Mr. Henry Strauss was a persistent enquirer over the possibility of stopping motor traffic on 'greenways' such as the Berkshire Ridgeway. The Bill, as drafted, enabled the Minister of Transport, on submission of a County or County Borough Council to make an Order restricting traffic on grounds of amenity in respect of a road in a National Park or Area of Outstanding Natural Beauty, or a road forming part of a long-distance path; it also gave the M.O.T. a default power on submission of the National Parks Commission in regard to roads in Parks or special areas. Strauss was worried about 'greenways' in other areas, but there was little the Minister could do on this point.

But the Minister successfully eased fears about compensation payable by landowners and injuries to ramblers on access land (for example from bulls). The Ministry of Fuel and Power, initially alarmed at the prohibitive cost of installing cables underground, were quietened when it became clear that there was no intention of causing exceptional expense to fall upon the Boards or consumers. Objection from the Forestry Commission about the proposal that woodland should not be excepted from public access was accompanied by criticisms during both Committee and Report stage, but the Minister held firm on this point after a new definition was agreed with the Forestry Commission. Water undertaking land was also the cause of close examination. In the end, the British Waterworks Association were satisfied with an amendment which provided that where a water undertaking objected to the inclusion of certain land in an Access Order on the grounds that it would involve danger to the purity of the water supply, its representations would be considered jointly by the Minister of Town and Country Planning before the Order was confirmed or made.

The National Parks and Access to the Countryside Act, 1949, received the Royal Assent in December. It made provision for the establishment of a National Parks Commission and for the designation of National Parks. It conferred on the Nature Conservancy and local authorities powers for the establishment and maintenance of Nature Reserves. It made further provision for the recording, creation, maintenance and improvement of public paths and for securing access to open country; the law relating to rights of way was amended. General powers were given to local planning authorities and there were further powers for preserving and enhancing natural beauty; the National Parks Commission might designate Areas of Outstanding Natural Beauty. Nineteen years had elapsed since the Addison Report of 1931; two decades of pressure from interest groups, Ministerial investigation and reports from appointed

Committees had finally come to fruition. Although the Act applied only to England and Wales, legislation for Scotland was expected to follow. In fact there were to be no National Parks for Scotland (see Chapter 8), but in 1949 there could reasonably be grounds for considerable satisfaction in many quarters.

CHAPTER 6

The Experiences of the National Parks Act: England and Wales during the Fifties

THIS chapter is largely concerned with the operation of the 1949 Act over the first ten years. It deals particularly with the issue of Park administration, especially the conflict over the setting up of Joint Boards and Park Committees and the continued pull between national and local interests; the subsequent approaches to the Minister as to desirable amendments to the legislation; and the Private Member's Bill introduced by Arthur Blenkinsop in 1958 to amend the 1949 Act. This is an Official History, and the chapter does not set out to review progress on the implementation of the Act (the designation of National Parks, expenditure on Park facilities, creation of long-distance footpaths or on the footpath survey for example), or to evaluate in any way the performance of the National Parks Commission. The elements of the wider story are chronicled elsewhere. But in order to describe certain Government and Departmental activities, it is necessary to touch on certain background amenity questions and other issues of national development which had their bearing on attitudes to National Park administration and the effectiveness or otherwise of the 1949 Act.

Administration of National Parks

It was not long before those who were suspicious of undue local interests overriding national considerations began to express concern over the future of Joint Boards as the organisational key to National Park administration. H. G. Griffin, now honorary secretary of the Standing Committee on National Parks, wrote to Hugh Dalton, Minister of Local Government and Planning, in August 1951 about the staffing and financing of the National Park Joint Boards.[108] Dalton, replying in September, said he felt there was no need for anxiety. Two Boards, for the Lakes and the Peak, had recently been set up, and experience should be allowed to show the way to go: ... 'this constant crying that the 1949 Act won't work and can't work before we have had a chance to try it, is the worst possible thing for the movement we all have at heart; and I believe your Committee's best contribution to the Parks would be for them to concentrate their interest on what needs to be done on the Parks instead of worrying whether the machinery will be adequate.'

True to style, Griffin wrote to the new Minister of Housing and Local Government, Harold Macmillan, in November. The Minister's reply followed his predecessor's advice. 'It seems to me to be proper to leave the newly constituted Boards to decide for themselves how they shall be staffed. They must be allowed to be the judges of what staff and what kind of staff is necessary. If I were to find, in due course, that their staffing arrangements were proving less than adequate, I should not hesitate to urge or, indeed, impose changes upon them, but I have no reason to anticipate such a situation.'

But the question was not to be avoided quite so easily. Dr. B. Stross brought forward the subject of National Parks at an Adjournment Debate on 6 December 1951 and spoke mainly on the staffing of Joint Boards. Two years had now elapsed since the passing of the 1949 Act, and there had been a change of Government. It was an appropriate time to begin to recall the assurances made during the passage of the National Parks Bill through the House, and to test the position of the new Administration. This was an important point and the basis of debate for some years.

Section 8 (2) of the National Parks Act provided that where a National Park lies within the area of more than one local planning authority 'there shall be a joint planning board under Section 4 of the Act of 1947 for a united district consisting of the area of the Park'. The Minister, however, could dispense with a Joint Board where, on the representation of any of the planning authorities affected and after consultation with the Commission, he was satisfied it was expedient so to do in order to secure efficient Park administration. The implication was clearly that it was going to be very difficult for the separate authorities to demonstrate that they could secure better administration of Park areas than could Joint Boards. The powers of a Joint Board when constituted were extensive: the Boards exercised all the functions of a planning authority for the area, preparing Development Plans and exercising day to day planning control. Where there was no Joint Board the individual planning authorities were obliged to set up a separate planning committee for the Park area and to delegate planning powers to such a committee. During the passage of the Bill the supporters of the National Parks and Open Air movements pressed strongly for single planning authorities, requiring a common policy throughout each Park and a common standard of administration. On the other hand local authorities were known not to like Joint Boards since it meant handing over some of their powers to a body on which they had a comparatively small representation.

The National Parks lobby also urged that there should be one planning officer and one staff dealing with the whole Park. The insistence on the separate planning officer grew when it became clear during the passage of the National Parks Bill that the Government had decided to place the responsibility for administering National Parks a good deal more in the hands of local authorities than the Hobhouse Committee had recommended. Silkin took the line that the Government, having inaugurated County Councils and County Borough Councils as local planning authorities with greatly strengthened powers, could not proceed to create different local planning authorities for the Parks, and that Joint Boards with two thirds membership coming from the local authorities concerned should be the normal machinery. The amenity bodies then sought to retrieve the position by various safeguards, including a proviso that each Board should have its own planning officer and other staff.

Mr. A. Greenwood, as one of the spokesmen for the amenity interests, raised this matter in Committee and there was certainly ambiguity in the subsequent proceedings. On the face of them an undertaking appeared to have been given, although later the Ministry preferred to argue that Silkin had applied himself to a different point. Subsequently, as we have seen, both Dalton and Macmillan held that the question whether or not there should be a planning officer ought to be left to the discretion of the Board. Once established, the National Parks Commission strongly favoured a separate planning officer.

The circumstances in which Dr. Stross was allotted the adjournment on 6 December 1951 were that the Peak Board had made an interim appointment of a part-time planning officer (previously the planning officer of the Peak area of Derbyshire C.C.), but the Lakes Board were so far divided on the matter. The amenity interests were looking at the situation closely, because they felt that officers still attached to the constituent Councils of the Park areas would continue to serve the interests of their Councils against the interest of the Joint Board.

The administrative tidying-up during the passage of the Bill soon looked unlikely to stand the test of time. The Lake District National Park followed the Peak in accepting, under Ministerial pressure, the administrative formula of a Joint Board, but decided to use the joint services of the county planning officers for Lancashire, Cumberland and Westmorland, for a trial period of three years. The Lakes County Councils also insisted that there should be a limit to what the Board could spend without reference back to their constituent Councils. The Department succeeded in raising this amount to £7,500 p.a., but the desire for economy was matched by a determination to keep effective Council control.[109]

The situation in Snowdonia also led to difficulties. There, the three County Councils pressed their desire not to have a Joint Board, but the Minister (Dalton) insisted that there were no exceptional circumstances to warrant him not following the normal requirement.

He wrote to the three Welsh counties on 4 June 1951: 'there can be no doubt that a Joint Board will be necessary in Snowdonia. . . . The Minister is clear there are no such exceptional circumstances in Snowdonia as would warrant him in dispensing with this requirement.'[110] The Order designating the Park became operative on 20 November 1951, but with a change of Government the new Minister (Macmillan) soon received a deputation from the Councils. This was on 26 March 1952, the outcome being that the Minister agreed to the establishment of a Joint Advisory Committee as an alternative arrangement, subject to assurances that such an arrangement would secure the efficient administration of the Park for an experimental period of three years. Macmillan's letter of 25 April 1952 confirmed this step.

With regard to the Pembroke Coast and Dartmoor National Parks, each lay within one county, and therefore administration was in the hands of a special Park Committee responsible direct to the County Council. In Dartmoor, however, there was a dispute as to the composition of the Committee. The National Parks Commission submitted a list of eight names for representatives, expressing a preference for the first six. Devon County Council asked to be consulted, and proceeded to omit two of the first six names on the grounds that they did not know them, but that they did know the others. When this became known it was attacked on the principle that the local authority already had two-thirds representation on the Committee, and that to allow them a say in the appointment of the remainder was to dilute the national representation.

In the summer of 1952 the whole question of the administration of the Parks came under renewed scrutiny. The Standing Committee on National Parks sent a deputation to the Minister on 26 May.*[111] They expressed disappointment at the failure of the last Government to implement the recommendations of the Hobhouse Report which would have secured the 'national' element in Park administration, and fell back on the various assurances wrung from the Minister in the course of the Bill through Parliament. The Committee argued that the Minister had given categorical assurances that Joint Boards would be set up save in exceptional circumstances, that every Board would have its own Planning Officer, and that Boards would not be obliged to go back to their constituent councils for necessary finances. They pointed to the situation in Snowdonia (over

---

* Consisting of J. W. Major (Acting Chairman), Sir Patrick Abercrombie, G. G. Haythornthwaite (Vice Chairman Peak District National Park Joint Planning Board), Mrs. Sylvia Sayer (member, Dartmoor National Park Planning Committee), Rev. H. H. Symonds (member, Lake District National Park Joint Planning Board) and H. G. Griffin (Hon. Secretary).

the Joint Board), to the Lake District (over the Planning Officer) and to Dartmoor (over Committee composition). The Minister rejoined by emphasising the purpose of National Parks: why bother about machinery? But the amenity interests saw only one road to salvation, and their pressure continued. Parliamentary opportunity was afforded in the Adjournment Debate of 8 July when Mr. A. Blenkinsop was a speaker and in the Supplies Debate of 14 July when both Blenkinsop and Greenwood spoke.[112]

The Minister bowed to local authority pressure over the question of Joint Boards and no more were created. The Joint Advisory Committee Order was made for Snowdonia on 9 February 1953, and in 1956 the arrangement was extended for another three experimental years. In the meantime experience elsewhere showed the strength of local authority feeling on National Park issues. The Commission's proposal for an Exmoor National Park for example met with a bleak reception. Neither Devon nor Somerset accepted the need for a Park on the grounds that its national beauty was already adequately protected under the 1947 Act. There was no reconciliation of divergent views and the Commission proceeded with designation, although the Quantocks were omitted from the designated area. As the Commission explained, 'it was separated from the designated area by a tract of country which was not of sufficient scenic quality to be included, and the Commission did not desire to add to the doubts of the County Council by including what might be considered to be an additional complication'.[113] A further concession was made in that a Joint Advisory Committee was allowed instead of a Joint Board, as was the case with the Yorkshire Dales National Park at about the same time (1956).

Proposals for the Amendment of the 1949 Act

In July 1955 the new Minister of Housing and Local Government, Duncan Sandys, invited the National Parks Commission to provide him with preliminary views on possible amendments of the 1949 Act. The time had come to evaluate the provisions of the Act in the light of evidence of their effectiveness. The Chairman, Lord Strang, submitted his recommendations on 2 February 1956.[114] He had nine proposals:

1. All expenditures incurred by the Park Planning Authorities in the exercise of powers made available by s.11 of the 1949 Act should be grant earning: these would include the setting up of information centres, publicity campaigns, and anti-litter action.
2. The limitation then imposed by sub-section 3 of s.11 upon the general powers granted by sub-section 1 of that section should be removed. There had been specific instances where action for

amenity purposes had been held up by the terms of this sub-section. For example when a Park planning authority asked a health authority to install litter bins at a much visited view point, the answer was that as the Park authority wanted the bins for amenity purposes, the cost of provision, and litter collection, should fall on them. This was prevented by s.11 (3). The removal of the limitation would also enable the Park authority to create new paths, maintain paths and pay compensation.

3. The limitation of the grant to 75% should be removed. It should be made possible for grant to be paid at amounts up to 100%. The Commission had no doubt that the need to find 25% of any contemplated grant-aided expenditure acted as a deterrent to positive action by Park planning authorities.

4. There should be provision for grant towards the administrative expenses of National Parks.

5. There should be provision for grant for administrative expenses incurred by local authorities on the administrative work involved in completing Long Distance Footpaths.

6. There should be provision for compensation to developers in National Parks and Areas of Outstanding Natural Beauty on whom the Park authority had imposed conditions involving additional expenditure because of a beautiful setting.

7. Planning authorities should have power to maintain a warden service, and grant should be payable on this expenditure.

8. The definition of 'waterway' given by s.114 (1) should include tidal and coastal waters. This was for access purposes, the Commission having in mind the possibility of improving facilities for sailing and boating at coastal sites.

9. The Commission should be enabled to place at the disposal of Park planning authorities the services not only of their own officers, but of expert advisers as consultants.

This was essentially a tidying-up operation together with a plea for greater financial support to be made available. The same line was followed in approaches to the Minister made by other bodies about this time. The Ramblers Association for example submitted a memorandum which broadly advocated measures recommended in the Hobhouse Report. Weightier representations made by deputations from the Park planning authorities and the County Councils Association (individually in April 1956, and jointly in February 1957) explored an old hopeful possibility, namely the use of the National Land Fund for National Park purposes. The Fund was set up by s.48 of the Finance Act, 1946, which set aside £50m. from which the Treasury could reimburse the Inland Revenue where property was accepted in satisfaction of death duties, and could then dispose of property to bodies such as the National Trust. The 1949 Act made no provision for using the National Land Fund, but the scope of the Fund was extended by the Finance Act, 1953, and the Historic Buildings and Ancient Monuments Act, 1953. This enabled the Ministry of Works to recover from the Fund the cost of acquiring or helping in the preservation of historic buildings. The Treasury always took the line that it was not appropriate for the Fund to be used for Park purposes, and in any case the use of the Fund in this way would involve amending the 1949 Act.

The time was not yet ripe for this step, and at a meeting with Lord Strang on 2 April 1957 Sandys made it clear that there was no hope of an amending Bill before 1959 at the earliest.[115] Proposals regarding National Parks had so far involved spending more money, and this Government could not yet countenance. The County Councils Association and the Park planning authorities had urged money to be available for expenditure in aid of higher standards, but the Minister was not to be moved.

Amenity and National Park Development

The National Parks lobby remained the intense interest of a small though vociferous minority. The Hobhouse Report was the essential reference point, and developments contrary to the hopes and intentions of that Report became the focus of sharp criticism. For example, failure to designate the Broads as a National Park (recommended by Hobhouse) did not go unnoticed. But the Commission argued that the Broads was an area of no outstanding beauty and its claim to National Park status was based on its value as a sailing ground. The sailing capacity was declining through silting and the Commission were not prepared to designate until they knew the scope of the remedial work necessary. Research by the Nature Conservancy was advocated, but no money was allocated for this. An entirely separate issue was the fact that the Broads lay astride Norfolk and Suffolk, and it was appreciated that problems could arise if a Joint Board were proposed.

On other matters the Commission found itself in conflict with the Ministry. A number of important development proposals were opposed by the Commission but supported by the Minister, and in attracting widespread public comment, they served to provide ammunition for the amenity bodies which claimed that the National Park interests were being sacrificed. This History does not examine how Government decisions on these projects came to be taken— that is a matter for further research at another time. But to provide a helpful context we should briefly mention some of these National Park developments because they contributed significantly to subsequent attitudes and pressures.

A proposed nuclear power station at Trawsfynydd in Snowdonia, to be situated on the shore of an artificial lake (required for cooling purposes), evoked a strong response from the Commission: 'The proposed power station, occupying, it seems, some 200 acres and including an outdoor switching compound, must, however well designed, remain a large and incongruous feature, and must be entirely out of place in a National Park. Not only so, but the over-head super-grid transmission lines required for connecting the station with the areas of consumption and with the grid . . . would necessarily pass over many miles of hill country and moorland of high quality.'[116] But on 31 July 1958, after a public local enquiry, the Minister of Power announced, after consultation with the Minister of Housing and Local Government, a decision to approve the C.E.G.B.'s application for both the station and the overhead lines.

Another contentious case concerned development at Milford Haven, where the British Petroleum Company had sought and obtained by Private Bill the right to construct an oil discharge installation on a site at Popton Point on the south shore of the Haven. This was within, albeit on the edge of, the Pembrokeshire National Park. The Esso Petroleum Company proposed a jetty and an oil refinery on a 900-acre site on the north shore of the Haven, two-thirds of which would lie within the National Park. Furthermore the Steel Company of Wales had plans for establishing an iron ore stocking ground at nearby Chapel Bay, well within the Park. The Commission found itself powerless over the British Petroleum Trading Bill. The Commission had no mandate to report direct to Parliament, and had no power to petition on a Private Bill. The Minister had agreed to reproduce as an appendix to any report which he made to Parliament on a Private Bill any advice which the Commission gave him. But the Bill was unopposed in Parliament and was therefore not examined by a Select Committee. Con-sequently the Commission's report was not taken into detailed Parliamentary consideration. The Commission had fears of a new sprawling industrial complex in this area, and (in respect of the iron ore stocking ground) they wrote of their 'deep concern at the fact that a site in the National Park should have been chosen for this project. We considered it to be totally at variance with the right use of land in a National Park.'[117] Planning approvals for the develop-ment, either wholly or in part, were forthcoming: the Minister felt that on the balance of advantages in the national interest he was not justified in refusing to grant planning permission.

Other issues contributed to a growing sense of unease by the Commission and the amenity interests. The Government decided with the U.S. Government to set up a Ballistic Missile Early Warning

Station at Fylingdales in the North York Moors. The Commission's view was that the 'decision to erect this installation was plainly inconsistent with the essential purposes of the National Parks Act'.[118] A second nuclear power station was required in North Wales and in July 1960 the Central Electricity Generating Board announced that they proposed to seek permission for development at Wylfra, Anglesey. The Annual Reports of the National Parks Commission faithfully record the balance sheet of successes and disappointments: stretches of electricity lines undergrounded, mineral workings resisted, successful negotiations with the Forestry Commission, the publication of the Country Code, and other benefits versus an inability to limit contentious Defence activities, lack of completion of long-distance routes, failure to arouse local authority enthusiasms, and sacrifice of amenity interests for other national developments in a number of important instances. In 1960 the Commission wrote of their 'profound disappointment at the number of occasions when National Park interests have had to be set aside in order to allow developments alien to the whole conception of National Parks'.[119]

Viewed in this way, it might be said that the high hopes of Dower, Hobhouse and Silkin had been scarcely met, and that the Commission had been disappointingly weak and ineffective. But on the other hand it is fair to point to solid achievement. Progress in the first ten years of the 1949 Act (1950–60) was represented by the confirmed designation of ten National Parks, totalling 5,258 sq. miles; 12 Areas of Outstanding Natural Beauty (1701 sq. miles); the publication of all draft maps and definitive maps for 14 counties and parts of three others, for public footpaths; the approval of three long-distance footpaths; and the completion by all authorities of Rights of Access Maps.

Above all, however, it is necessary to recognise that the general situation with regard to National Parks and countryside recreation was beginning to exhibit new features. The Commission itself admitted this very early on, remarking that 'we are living in an age of transition when, for the first time, a preponderantly urban population largely unfamiliar with rural life has acquired a considerable amount of leisure with the opportunity of using that leisure to satisfy the instinctive and wholesome desire to leave the city for the country. We cannot prevent this influx of town into country, nor on a long view of the healthy development of our nation, should we desire to prevent it'.[120] These new social developments began to change some important assumptions about National Parks and access to the countryside.

In the meantime one added spur might be recorded which aimed to provide new possibilities for public access to the countryside.

The Royal Commission on Common Land reported in 1958.[121] Set up in 1955 under the chairmanship of Sir William Ivor Jennings, it was asked 'to recommend what changes, if any, are desirable in the law relating to common land in order to promote the benefit of those holding manorial and common rights, the enjoyment of the public, or, where at present little or no use is made of such land, its use for some other desirable purpose'. Two recommendations at least were relevant to National Park and countryside considerations. It was recommended that the general restrictions on access to open country set out in the Second Schedule of the 1949 Act should apply to all common land (para. 318). It was also recommended that in addition to public rights of access for air and exercise, a local authority should be able to undertake a scheme for the management and improvement of common land to enhance public enjoyment still further (para. 329).

Private Member's Bill, 1959

The decade closed with a private member's attempt to obtain support for new National Parks legislation. In 1958 Arthur Blenkinsop was successful in winning 12th place in the ballot for Private Members' Bills, and intimated his intention of introducing a short measure to extend powers to make grants for National Park purposes broadly on the lines suggested by the Park planning authorities and the County Councils Association two years earlier. His Bill was to come up for Second Reading on 30 January 1959. The matter was discussed at Home Affairs Committee on 5 December 1958.

A Joint Memorandum by the Minister of Housing and Local Government, Henry Brooke, and the Financial Secretary to the Treasury, J. E. S. Simon, asked for guidance.[122] The Minister thought that the Bill would receive support from both sides of the House, and if the Government were to oppose it without suggesting that in due course it would provide for some new arrangement helpful to National Parks they would be friendless in the Press and in the House. But he felt it quite inappropriate to use the National Land Fund for National Park purposes. He was also against Blenkinsop's proposals to increase the 75% limit of grant. But he was sympathetic to other points, for example the proposal to provide grants (on the existing 75% basis) towards certain activities which did not then attract grant, and to extend the existing grant-aided warden service to any land to which the public had access *de facto* (it was then limited to land to which they had access *de jure*). The Minister said he had in mind to propose legislation for these purposes, though not within the life of the present Parliament. Blenkinsop had indicated that if the Government would assist him with the drafting of the Bill and provide a Financial Resolution, he would drop his proposal to use the

Land Fund. The maximum expenditure entailed, which would take a year or two to reach, was thought to be between £40–50,000 annually. The Minister anticipated popular credit if assistance were offered.

The Financial Secretary doubted whether the Government should allow itself to be driven into supporting the Bill. He thought that the local authorities responsible for National Parks were not shouldering a really heavy burden, and that in some cases tourist traffic was actually of benefit to them. He considered that the case for the extra expenditure was less strong than that of other claims which had had to be rejected. He agreed with the Minister that the device of using the National Land Fund was disreputable. In conclusion he agreed with the Minister that sympathy with the general aim of the Bill and an indication that the Government had it in mind to bring forward proposals of its own in the next Parliament would be helpful. He reminded his colleagues that National Parks were a unique local authority service—administered by a few local authorities almost wholly in the national and not the local interest.

The Home Affairs Committee[123] decided that the Bill should be opposed on the ground that it was constitutionally improper either for the Bill itself to impose a charge on the Exchequer through the device proposed, or for the Government to provide it with a Financial Resolution. If it proved impossible to defeat the Bill on Second Reading, it would be necessary to defeat it in Committee. The Home Affairs Committee did not follow the cautious suggestion of the Minister and the Secretary of State in holding out an indication of future Government legislation, and thought it preferable not to give any definite promise of Government legislation in a later Session.

Blenkinsop's Bill was published in January 1959: 'to make further provision concerning National Parks, to amend the National Parks and Access to the Countryside Act, 1949, to improve the administration of National Parks, to provide funds for this purpose from the National Land Fund; and for purposes connected with the matters aforesaid'. Apart from the omission of any provision to increase the maximum rate of grant payable for Park purposes from 75%, the Bill was in its expected form and contained amendments to the 1949 Act covering nine points. Most of the amendments proposed in 1956 by the National Parks Commission were included and its terms also covered the proposals submitted subsequently by the Park planning authorities and the County Councils Association.

The objections to the Bill remained. Constitutionally it was argued that a Private Member's Bill may not, in general, create a charge on public funds. Such Bills sometimes add by implication minor charges to public funds by way of administrative costs, and on such occasions the Government may provide a financial resolution, but Blenkinsop's Bill aimed to extend the range of grants by using the National Land Fund, and this remained unacceptable in principle. On the last occasion when the Public Accounts Committee considered the National Land Fund (in June 1958), the Treasury witness, Sir Thomas Padmore, affirmed the principle that the Fund should not be used to supplement provision made by Parliament by Votes. The second objection was that the extra expenditure, even though relatively trivial, could not be afforded. After the Home Affairs Committee in December the Treasury in correspondence with the Ministry appeared to move towards the idea that this in fact was the main argument against accepting the Bill.[124] The Ministry found difficulties in this point because the Treasury had been unable to produce any better priorities than proposals for a chiropodist service and a provision for higher grant for old people's homes. It was thought in the Ministry that if this was the preferred Treasury line it would make it difficult to claim that Government attached importance to the success of National Parks. The principle of using the National Land Fund was in fact the argument used to defeat the Bill: the Minister advised the House not to give it a Second Reading and Blenkinsop's measures were lost.

CHAPTER 7

The Review of Legislation: The Countryside Act, 1968

CONCERN over National Parks was increased rather than reduced by Blenkinsop's abortive measure, and over the next few years a combination of circumstances conspired to maintain pressure for new legislation. At first, the prospect was confined to a simple amending Bill, but from 1964 onwards the issue became one of a radically different Bill which sought to give effect to a comprehensive countryside policy. Three stages can be recognised: first, the period 1959–63 when the Ministry of Housing and Local Government reconsidered the merits of administrative reorganisation in the context of sustained pressure from the interest groups concerned; second, the period 1963–64 when a new outlook advanced the consideration of the future of National Parks to a new approach which included the countryside as a whole; and third, the period 1964–68 when a new Department, the Ministry of Land and Natural Resources, put forward the structure of a new Countryside Bill. The Countryside Act, 1968, became the successor to the National Parks Act, 1949.

1959–63

A memorandum from the Minister, Henry Brooke, to the Secretary of his Department in October 1959 asked for preparation to be put in hand for a National Parks Amendment Act 'sometime during this Parliament'.[125] The Conservative Administration had been returned and a new Parliamentary timetable could therefore be considered. Some sort of review of National Parks legislation would be required, and the events of the previous few years already suggested the headings under which a new Bill might be considered.

For some years the arguments continued on familiar lines. The crux of the matter seemed to be finance. The additional powers needed, or so far advocated, appeared comparatively minor. The problem was for more money to put new heart into the Park authorities. It was thought that information on expenditure obtained from Park authorities early in 1961 would show what needed to be done; it would provide the elements of a new case to Ministers and the Treasury and would enable the preparation of a new Bill. In the meantime it was expected that the National Parks Commission

E

would amplify the proposals made in 1956. Observations were also awaited from the Nature Conservancy. Suggestions had already been made by the County Councils Association, and these covered a number made by the Ramblers Association, the Youth Hostels Association, the Councils for the Preservation of Rural England and Wales, the National Farmers Union and the National Trust. With the aid of new information, particularly on finance, and assisted by fresh consultations, it was hoped to prepare a paper for the Home Affairs Committee by the end of May 1961, so as to have a reasonable chance of getting a Bill ready for introduction by the end of the year.

Along with finance the principal problem remained the local administration of the Park authorities. Many of the amenity and outdoor organisations still regretted the fact that the Hobhouse proposals were not given effect and thought that this was a reason for lack of progress in the preservation and enhancement of the Parks. But this was not to be an area of change. The Minister wanted a short and non-controversial amending Bill, and to alter the administrative arrangements in any way would be to plunge the Bill into controversy. He had no intention of doing that.

The National Parks Commission made its suggestions for the amendment of the 1949 Act in May 1961.[126] The Commission retained seven of their original nine proposals, though extending the scope in some cases. They added eight more. Consequently they were requesting a good deal more than in 1956: in particular they wanted Park activities to extend to Areas of Outstanding Natural Beauty with the extended grant aid suggested for Parks. The seven proposals retained were as follows:

> grant for extra administration,
> removal of the 75% limit on grant,
> grant for all expenditure on Park activities under s.11 of the
>   1949 Act,
> removal of the embargo under s.11,
> extension of the warden service,
> powers to employ expert advisers, and extension of powers to
>   enable works on the coast.

The two proposals now omitted were:

> provision for compensation to developers, and
> provision for grant for administration over long-distance paths.

The additional proposals were:

> wide powers of acquisition for Park authorities,
> grant on the maintenance and management of derelict land and
> tree planting schemes,

122

programmes of work for Areas of Outstanding Natural Beauty, powers to make byelaws and orders to control boating in Park areas, grants for repairs and renewals to buildings which form an important feature of beauty in Parks and Areas of Outstanding Natural Beauty,

transfer of the responsibility for creating new rights of way necessary to establish a long-distance route from district councils to county councils,

general powers to be given to the Commission in respect of long-distance routes similar to those they already had under s. 6 for National Parks, and

the Commission should have power to recommend the creation of rights of way by Park authorities in National Parks.

These recommendations from the National Parks Commission formed the most substantive representations which the Minister had to consider. But the emotional question of local versus national interests in Park administration continued to rumble. Arthur Hobhouse took the opportunity to write to the Minister in March 1961 with the agreement of former colleagues on his National Parks Committee: he was 'disturbed to hear of the demands by the District Councils for further local representation upon the National Park Planning authorities when already the local outweighs the national representation in the proportion of two-thirds to one-third; and even further weight is accorded to the local interest by a large degree of delegation of Part III Planning Powers'.[127] He went on to suggest that this weakness in National Park administration had led to failure in protecting National Parks from undesirable encroachments.

A deputation to the Minister from the Associations of the Urban District Councils and the Rural District Councils took place in July 1961.[128] They pressed for direct representation of district councils on Park planning boards and committees. In the past the main pressure for direct representation had come from the Rural District Councils Association (mainly at the instigation of Bakewell R.D.C. in the Peak District) but the Urban District Councils Association now associated themselves with the deputation (Bakewell U.D.C. having protested more actively than the R.D.C. over the last year). The point at issue may have been a local one but it was typical of wider sensitivities. Derbyshire County Council had made it a practice to appoint their members to the Park Planning Board from the majority party, with the consequence that their representatives tended to come from the industrial and mining areas away from the Peak. In 1957 the County Council were asked informally to remedy this situation and did so; with the appointment of a Bakewell Rural District Councillor the complaints ceased. However, he died in 1959 and was replaced by a Councillor from Heanor, whereupon the protests were resumed. Two petitions to the Queen followed in 1960 and 1961 from a Bakewell Urban District Councillor urging direct representation of the U.D.C. on the Peak Park Planning Board. This councillor was a member of the deputation to the Minister in July 1961.

Whatever sympathies might have been expressed about local difficulties, at no time was any indication given that the Minister was prepared to consider favourably any reform of the Park administrative structure. Any new National Parks legislation was to be on the basis of a fairly simple amending Bill concerned with financial provisions and other powers. None the less the question of direct representation of district councils (and other bodies) on National Park Planning Boards and committees continued to be the subject of correspondence and discussion. Indeed its importance was such that it tended to dominate the climate of thinking about the future of National Parks; with hindsight, it was a matter which received undue prominence, it contributed to a departmental despair at the single-minded parochial level of thinking of the amenity bodies, and it prejudiced more fundamental debate about National Park planning that was now demanded and overdue.

An example of the running battle between the district councils and the Minister was that in September 1962 the Lakes Urban District Council wrote to all 72 district councils in the National Parks asking for their support in putting the case for direct representation to the Minister.*[129] As a result 34 councils wrote to the Department. The Minister's replies made it clear that he thought that the appointment by the county council of two-thirds of the members of a Park Board or committee was adequate to secure representation of local interests; moreover he could not accept they could do little for local wishes.

In the meantime there had been no progress on amending the 1949 Act. The National Park Commissioners' revised proposals had been received, but the credit squeeze of 1961 had postponed any legislation. However, Ministers were on record in accepting the need for amendment: at each of the Annual Conferences of the National Park authorities, begun in 1959, Ministers had talked in these terms, though making it clear that there was no early propect of new legislation and without taking any firm decisions on its nature.

It is difficult to resist the view that Governmental thinking about National Parks and related aspects of recreation planning in the countryside had become ossified. Financial stringency made possible only modest possible extension of grant-aid; administrative reform

* Charles Hill replaced Henry Brooke on 9 October 1961; Sir Keith Joseph replaced Charles Hill on 13 July 1962.

of the Park planning system was not to be contemplated; the Department and the Commission maintained an uneasy relationship in the borderland of interest between national land use considerations and the principles of amenity protection. The Commission was known to be a weak body, having the obligation to recommend and represent on so many subjects but the power to act on so few. The Park Planning authorities had done well in maintaining high standards of development control, but had done little (with the exception of the Peak Board) on the management side. In England, of the projects approved for grant by the end of 1962, car parks and lay-bys outnumbered everything else.*[130] The local authorities were poor spenders, but there were staff difficulties (only the Peak Board had a separate staff with a full time planning officer). With regard to Areas of Outstanding Natural Beauty, the efforts had related almost entirely to development control standards; Cannock Chase was exceptional in its management schemes and warden service.

In this context, the outlook in relation to new legislation was confined to extension of grant aid and to a variety of suggestions for strengthening the performance of the Commission, such as through enhancing its public image and improving its staff complement. Even so, there is little evidence of either political will or Departmental enthusiasm for securing what seemed desirable. The officials observed that in spite of all the protests from the rural counties, the 75% grant rate was not ungenerous. All the Park authorities received rate deficiency grant, and the poorest authorities received a 50% rate, implying that their effective rate of grant was only just under 90%. Another reaction was for the Department to criticise the Commission, considering that they never sought to make maximum use of their powers. All this led to a general conclusion, therefore, that what was wanted in relation to National Parks was not so much greatly increased powers, but a more effective application of those existing, although it was accepted that there were certain fresh legislative provisions which could be made with advantage. But above all, the focus of thinking remained on National Parks and the working of the 1949 Act; there was as yet no widening of a view, and no recognition of a different problem, that could provide a different base for new legislation.

---

* Car parks or lay-bys	: 68, of which 14 were in the Peak Park		
camping, caravan sites or picnic areas	: 7,	,, 3	,,
tree planting	: 16,	,, 5	,,
purchase of woodlands	: 7,	,, 7	,,
clearance of eyesores/ improvement of derelict land	: 13,	,, 4	,,
hostels—new	: 1		
—conversions	: 2,	,, 1	,,
warden service	: 5,	,, 1	,,

Towards the end of 1962, though more clearly at the end of 1963, the National Parks question began to take on this new dimension. An enlarged awareness and a new scale of thinking emerged. The origins were in part related to a developing set of academic and other enquiries in this country, and particularly in North America, which was beginning to examine a range of countryside and recreation matters extending beyond the previous concern of National Parks.* In Government circles the new interest in outdoor leisure was stimulated by the speculation aroused by the Countryside in 1970 Conference held in November 1963. The Minister, Sir Keith Joseph, was noticeably keener to take new initiatives than his two predecessors, and the whole situation changed with surprising suddenness.

The period began conventionally enough. On 30 November 1962 Mr. Jeremy Thorpe inaugurated a Parliamentary debate on National Parks with the motion, 'That this House congratulates the National Parks Commission on their progress over the past 13 years in furthering the purposes set out in the National Parks and Access to Countryside Act, 1949; considers that time has shown the need for amendment of the Act in a number of respects, so as to facilitate the extension and diversification of the activities of the Commission and, particularly, with regard to the existing financial arrangements; and urges Her Majesty's Government to introduce amending legislation accordingly'.[131] But there were soon to be indications that the time was considered ripe for change. Mr. F. Corfield, a Parliamentary Secretary to the Minister, considered in December that there should be a White Paper on Government thinking on the lines of amending the 1949 Act.[132] In January 1963 Sir Keith Joseph asked the Departmental Secretary, Dame Evelyn Sharp, whether it was not possible to bring the Bill forward.[133]

Talks with the National Parks Commission were once again necessary and on 27 March 1963 the Minister himself attended a meeting with the Commission.[134] There is evidence from this meeting of a readiness to speculate about new possibilities concerning National Parks and the countryside. For example, Sir Keith Joseph floated a private idea of 'recreational areas'—areas of intensive open-air activities, not in National Parks, but planned to draw people away from areas of quietude. He went on to talk about a recreation policy for these areas.

A new political initiative was taken, although there could be no promise of early action. At the Future Legislation Committee in April 1963 a National Parks Bill was ranked in Category C. But

---

* Notably the work of the Outdoor Recreation Resources Review Commission in the U.S.A., and its series of study reports published in 1962.

Joseph was determined to activate a situation which had remained dormant for too long. This he did by exposing an unsatisfactory situation, suggesting by implication that things would have to change. At the Scarborough Conference of Park planning authorities in May 1963 he revealed that up to March 1962, the ten Park authorities had spent £114,000 in ten years on grant-aided activities. Of this just on £80,000 was spent by the two Boards, leaving under £40,000, in ten years spent by the eight other Park authorities. 'The sum total of accommodation, camping sites and the like provided by the other eight National Park Authorities amounts to one hostel built and another planned, one chalet scheme under way, a few car parks and small lay-bys provided.'[135]

After the Minister's meeting with the Commission, the Department continued the negotiations to explore the ground on which amending legislation would be acceptable. The Department pursued a number of objectives:[136]

1. to strengthen the local administration of the Parks by ensuring that the Park authorities were better staffed and had sufficient financial independence;
2. to introduce a new, simple and comprehensive grants scheme;
3. to strengthen the Commission; and
4. to extend some powers of the Park authorities and the Commission.

The Department saw as very important the creation of Joint Boards as the Park Authorities in the four 'multi-county' Parks which had refused initially to appoint them. (As the Minister had implied at Scarborough, the County Councils were simply not spending money, whereas the Joint Boards were.) Additionally, they recognised the need to contribute to administrative costs in all Parks.

In August 1963 a Departmental memorandum to the Commission suggested the following elements in new legislation:

1. provision for setting up new style National Park authorities;
2. provision for grant to be paid towards the extra administrative costs of the National Park authorities;
3. to abolish designation by the Commission of Areas of Outstanding Natural Beauty, but to provide for these areas to be shown in Development Plans with an explanation of development control policy;
4. application of present grants to these Areas;
5. extension of powers—for example, powers attracting grant, extension of definition of 'waterway' etc;
6. introduction of a new grant system.

The Commission indicated that they would support much of

this. In particular, they liked the idea of establishing Boards in all the Parks, and they welcomed the promise of change in procedure for the designation of Areas of Outstanding National Beauty, because of the relief it would entail from a great deal of detailed work. The Treasury appeared satisfied, but further contact with the Ministry of Science was still needed because of changes then in mind concerning the Nature Conservancy. The two major hurdles remained the difficulty of fitting the Bill into the Parliamentary programme and the obligation to consult Local Authority Associations. By November 1963 a letter had been drafted to the County Councils Association explaining the new legislative proposals.

Second thoughts soon prevailed. By the beginning of 1964 the Department recognised that the administrative proposals would not do. In each of the four Parks managed by Joint Advisory Committees (Brecon, Exmoor, Snowdonia and the Yorkshire Dales) the Minister had already expressed himself satisfied that owing to special circumstances Joint Boards were unnecessary. The working of the Joint Advisory Committees had been reviewed after a trial period, and they had been allowed to continue. An opposite view now was scarcely justified. Another argument for caution was the recognition that in the four single County Parks (Dartmoor, Northumberland, North Yorkshire Moors and Pembroke) there were already single authorities with all the necessary powers. Accordingly the draft letter to the County Councils Association was amended: now it was proposed to take power to appoint special authorities for the single County Parks should that prove desirable. But this letter was not sent either, and it seemed that once again an impasse had been reached.

An ever increasing problem was that the present Administration was nearing the end of its Parliamentary life, and the likelihood was that it would be impossible to proceed with any amending legislation. The Minister asked for a report to go to the Home Affairs Committee early in 1964. Drafts were prepared for March and again for April, but it was a lame document, and was in fact never submitted.[137] The memorandum briefly reviewed progress during the past 15 years and pointed to two needs: one to make Joint Boards obligatory for all the multi-county parks, and one to provide additional Exchequer grant for the Park authorities. But it was admitted that the proposed changes would be highly controversial, with the county councils resisting attempts to take Park administration out of their hands. The memorandum concluded that the Bill would be contentious and troublesome, and therefore it would not be a suitable measure to bring forward at that time.

But the memorandum did hint at a new dimension of the National Park question, namely the pressures on the countryside generally, arising from a rapidly growing urban population with more money and more leisure time. It was admitted that these questions merited further study and that it would be wise to think in terms of legislation on a wider front covering both the protection of the countryside and its use for recreation and leisure.

For the first time, in a report provisionally destined for a Cabinet Committee, the fruits are seen of new Ministerial thinking about a comprehensive view concerning countryside recreation planning. For many years a Bill had not been prepared because of low political priorities and obstacles over extension of grant aid. Now, when circumstances suggested that these difficulties might be removed, there seemed to be fresh reasons for caution. These were related to an unsureness as to what to legislate for; suddenly there seemed new questions to ask. A Departmental note at the end of 1963 from W. F. B. Lovett to the Chief Planner, J. R. James,[138] indicated these, giving the first evidence of a fresh approach away from the sterile debate about grant aid and administrative structures. The Countryside in 1970 Conference in November 1963 organised by the Nature Conservancy to enquire into problems of conservation and management of rural areas had surged with new viewpoints, to the extent that there was some bewilderment as to what the next steps should be. Publication in March 1964 extended the debate.[139] A unity of approach to countryside problems, with an administrative machine shaped to the job, became compelling; relevance was seen in recent Departmental work concerning coastal preservation,* the review of green belts and work on village growth. Lovett's note suggested that new legislation should retain the National Parks Commission, though with broader functions and perhaps a new name. It would be an advisory body to Park Boards and local planning authorities covering new landscape and amenity issues, and undertaking advisory and research work on recreation demands and provisions.

A new framework for thinking had been fashioned. For the first time there was by implication a re-examination of the assumptions underlying the Hobhouse Report. The Hobhouse Committee had done their work in 1945–47, and their thinking had been influenced by an assumption about a resumption of pre-war trends and a countryside as envisaged in the Scott Report. But some very different changes had taken place. There had been a steady and considerable population increase (and its further extension was forecast) accompanied by higher space standards for many facilities. A vast increase in car and caravan ownership (and hence of personal mobility) had taken place. There had been an increase in leisure time and all

---

* M.H.L.G. Circular 56/63.

forms of recreation. Tourism was now important in the national economy. Changes had taken place in forestry and in agricultural practice. Control over land use was generally effective under the Town and Country Planning Act, 1947. Approaching two decades after Hobhouse there should be a readjustment of policy to current conditions.

As suggested in the draft memorandum to the Home Affairs Committee in April 1964, the Minister was keen to press for a comprehensive view of countryside recreation. He accepted that a National Parks Bill should not be rushed, but was attracted by the idea of a comprehensive policy in relation to the countryside. But he was held back by the Departmental Secretary. Dame Evelyn Sharp warned Sir Keith Joseph in April that ideas on countryside aspects that were wider than National Parks were not yet worked out, and suggested that 'The whole subject has the danger anyway that it could open up an amenity clamour for Exchequer money'. The Minister thought that the wider ideas might be put to a Committee. Dame Evelyn thought that this would look like 'death bed repentance'. It would not be right for Government to appoint a Committee so near to the end of Parliament; 'there was great danger of a Committee running wild'.[140]

No formal Committee was established but in July the Minister consulted with a number of Planning Officers* on the adequacy of present machinery (legislative, administrative and financial) for the demands that were likely to be made upon it, and how the machinery might be supplemented. In the meantime Joseph had taken the opportunity in May at the Tenby National Park authorities' Conference to give a clear indication of what changes the future might bring:

'The first reflection that occurs to me is to wonder whether it makes sense to compartmentalise the countryside in the way that we tend to do. There are the National Parks—and the long-distance routes— and their Commission—and with some power and some financial resources only for them; then there are the areas of outstanding natural beauty controlled within normal planning power by the local planning authorities. And then there is the rest of the country-side—much of it of great beauty: all of it within planning control.

'If we are to adopt a positive policy for the countryside is this the best way to do it? And should we not have a positive policy for the countryside?

'Let me make it clear—no Government can find large additional sums of money for all desirable objectives. But might it not be that all sorts of existing programmes and all sorts of existing activities could be better harmonised with the countryside if there were a body

* Messrs P. Turnbull, A. D. G. Smart, E. H. Doubleday, R. C. Maxwell and J. Foster.

responsible, expert, devoted but not fanatic—available to advise local planning authorities, to discuss with farmers, to deal with every sort of interest group and to help the Government?

'Of course we need to keep the special provisions for National Parks but does it follow that we have to limit the National Parks Commission either in name or in deed only to their present scope? Have we not in the Commission the seed of a body with wider scope—the interests of the countryside as a whole?'[141]

A change of Administration took place in October 1964. By that time it was clear that future legislation on National Parks was going to be on a very different basis from that explored on several occasions between 1956 and 1963. Both the Labour and Conservative Parties in their Election Manifestoes were committed to legislation which would place emphasis on promoting outdoor recreation (the existing National Parks Act was primarily concerned with preservation). The Conservatives proposed 'to set up a Countryside Commission with sufficient resources to secure the positive care of the countryside and coast including the National Parks. . . . While strictly safeguarding secluded areas, the Commission will advise planning authorities on the designation of recreation areas where boating, climbing, gliding and similar activities will be welcomed'. The Labour Party undertook to 'preserve access to the coast and protect it from pollution and unplanned development'.

The situation was ready-made for change. The issues had changed sharply over the past year. There were new assumptions and therefore it was possible to think in terms of new needs being met by new powers. A totally new Act was required, not simply an amendment of the 1949 Act. What was most needed was further powers to provide new facilities for recreation. There was a need for a range of basic facilities and services: rights of access and use, development of recreation potential (particularly water), and provision for cars, toilets, litter bins and so on. This was particularly so where there was good country near large centres of population and along the coast; only in National Parks did local planning authorities have powers to provide facilities for the public enjoyment of the countryside. Provision for securing public access was country-wide, but was only grant aided in National Parks and Areas of Outstanding Natural Beauty. Finally there was no provision in National Parks or elsewhere which enabled local planning authorities to buy areas of open country and manage them for public benefit.

With regard to the Commission in the new situation, it had no claim to be a specialist body. Three members had specialist qualifications (in geography, archaeology and zoology); the rest were public spirited people with an interest in National Park affairs. Yet because the staff was little more than a secretariat, most of the work was done by the Commissioners, individually or collectively. A new kind of Commission was required, less amateur and more specialist, and more interested in wider opportunities for recreation.

Changing outlooks posed further questions, not previously raised. If a comprehensive countryside policy were to be the aim, then it had to be admitted that countryside questions were no one Department's responsibility, split as they were between the Ministry of Housing and Local Government, Department of Education and Science, Board of Trade, Ministry of Transport and the Ministry of Agriculture, Fisheries and Food. A reorganisation of Departmental functions might well be necessary.

There were the points raised in a Departmental note from J. E. Beddoe to the Deputy Secretary in October 1964.[142] The firm conclusion was that tinkering with the National Parks Act was no longer adequate to deal with the problem. What was needed was a policy for planning land uses to meet the needs of the populations of the large towns: it was necessary to plan for the countryside just as for the urban areas. Over the last two years and particularly over the last nine months the National Parks question had changed considerably.

1964–68

Consequent upon the creation of the Ministry of Land and Natural Resources in November 1964, responsibility for National Parks was transferred to the new Ministry, while responsibility for the countryside outside the National Parks remained with the Ministry of Housing and Local Government. M.H.L.G. remained responsible for planning in England, including National Parks, and retained responsibility for Areas of Outstanding Natural Beauty and access to the countryside. M.L.N.R. became responsible for the National Parks Commission and appointment of its members. It was responsible for those aspects of National Parks except planning: that is, including payment of Exchequer grants, access to open country, long distance footways and bridleways and nomination of the non-elective members of the Planning Boards and committees of the Parks. In Wales and Monmouth the planning function was the responsibility of the Secretary of State for Wales; he shared with the Minister L.N.R. oversight of Offa's Dyke long-distance path, which traversed both sides of the Border. The Nature Conservancy was now the responsibility of the Natural Environmental Research Council.

The new Ministry set to work on proposals for a new Bill. The auguries were favourable. The recent upsurge of enthusiasm for comprehensive countryside policies both within and outside Government was bringing a change of outlook within the National Parks

Commission itself. A new Principal Planning Officer, R. J. S. Hook-way, was appointed in February 1965, and a technical planning branch was set up in the Commission to co-ordinate studies of the coast and of the National Parks with the planning authorities. As previously noted, the American study*, which led to the setting up of the Bureau of Outdoor Recreation, and the beginnings of British research into leisure and use of the countryside pointed conclusively to rapidly expanding demands for open air recreation. They also pointed to the need for comprehensive countryside planning in terms of both provision of new facilities in selected areas and of management of resources. In the light of all these factors the Commission was happy to echo the need for a more authoritative body than the Commission then was.[143]

The new Minister, F. T. Willey, soon declared his hand. At the Harrogate Conference of Park planning authorities in May 1965 he gave clear indications, just as Sir Keith Joseph had done earlier at Tenby, of what he had in mind. 'Today we cannot rest content to repair the shortcomings of the 1949 Act. Today, we need to look beyond the boundaries of the National Parks; we need a more comprehensive and ambitious countryside policy.'[144]

A note to other Departments was circulated by the Ministry of Land and Natural Resources in June 1965.[145] It proposed to bring up-to-date the law dealing with the use of the countryside for recreation and rename the National Parks Commission as the Countryside Commission. It suggested a new facility 'countryside recreation sites'—places of 'up to, say, 20 acres, or even considerably more in particular circumstances, which would be kept in a more or less natural state, where cars could be parked in a reasonably dispersed manner among trees and bushes, but where lavatories and arrangements for dealing with litter could be provided'; they might be on National Parks, Areas of Outstanding Natural Beauty and in the countryside at large. The advantage of water in these sites was stressed. The note went on to outline the facilities that would attract grant.

With regard to the preservation of amenity it was proposed to strengthen the role of the Commission in two novel ways. First it was proposed that the Commission should have power, in consultation with county councils, to designate on development plans Areas of Outstanding Natural Beauty and other areas of special landscape beauty. Second, concern was expressed about the preservation of coastal amenities, and it was proposed to define a category of 'coastal areas', to which all the facilities applicable to Areas of Outstanding Natural Beauty would also apply, but where the

---

* *Report of the Outdoor Recreation Resources Review Commission*, 1962.

influence or control of the Commission over planning development should be somewhat stronger. It was suggested that in 'coastal areas' the local planning authorities should be obliged to consult the Commission over the current state of their development plan and over any development projects which were not in accordance with the current development plan as approved by the Commission.

There was a striking development in the proposals outlined in this note from all previous suggestions for new legislation. The combination of a change of Government, the creation of a new Department and the assembly of Departmental staff was a powerful impetus towards new speculative proposals. It brought an inevitable reaction from the Ministry of Housing and Local Government: in particular to the suggestion that the Commission should have power to designate Areas of Outstanding Natural Beauty. The observation was that the Development Plan procedure would be slower and more cumbersome than previously. Moreover, it was considered odd that the attempt to introduce stronger central control was being suggested precisely at a time when attempts were being made to move the other way. The recent Report of the Planning Advisory Group had advocated less central control over local planning issues.*[146]

Mr. Willey quickly followed this note by presenting his Memorandum to the Home Affairs Committee in July 1965.[147] He sought approval for the preparation of new legislation and for the publication of proposals in a White Paper in the autumn. His proposals were concerned with the use and conservation of the countryside, making provision for basic facilities, including land and water, for relaxation in and enjoyment of the countryside. The intention would be to broaden the scope of the National Parks policy, notably by providing for sites for recreation anywhere outside built up areas, and by giving financial assistance for a wide range of purposes outside, and not merely within National Parks and Areas of Outstanding Natural Beauty. He described his ideas for extending grant to 'countryside recreation sites'. With regard to the preservation of amenities he accepted that the Minister of Housing and Local Government, R. H. S. Crossman, was then examining the current planning system: he introduced a personal view that regional boards might be given responsibility for some broad designation of land use, including designation for amenity and recreation purposes. He accepted the criticism received on Areas of Outstanding Natural Beauty and compromised in a suggestion that the Commission should have power, in consultation with county councils, to propose 'special amenity areas' for designation on Development Plans. With extension of grant facilities it was thought that the cost of proposals,

---

* *The Future of Development Plans*, H.M.S.O., 1965.

134

which would not arise until 1967–68 would be between £1–2 million, to be fixed annually in consultation with the Treasury.

An accompanying Memorandum[148] by the Secretary of State for Education and Science, C. A. R. Crosland, questioned whether it would not be right to give grant aid to recreation facilities in urban areas if they were to be given in the countryside on the scale proposed. Balance between urban and rural provision had to be considered.

More important was a Memorandum[149] by R. H. S. Crossman who agreed that a clearer policy towards the use of the countryside for leisure and recreation was needed, but did not think Mr. Willey's paper gave such a policy. There was no indication as to what the £1–2 million a year would be spent on. Mr. Crossman's Department was studying green belts and coastal areas, and he hoped that he and Mr. Willey could submit a joint paper with the Minister of Sport, D. Howell, covering the whole subject of the use of the countryside for recreation. He thought their collective ideas should be worked out before presenting them in a White Paper.

In discussion, further grounds for interdepartmental consultation were given. For example, it was necessary to avoid any appearance of conflict with proposals then being considered for Rural Development Boards in upland areas, with their own responsibility for recreation and tourism. Secondly there was the need to consult the Ministry of Transport in view of their concern with the use of inland waterways. In conclusion Willey was asked to preside over a small sub-committee of Ministers concerned, supported by an interdepartmental working party of officers, to deal with the issues raised.

The matter came back to Home Affairs Committee in October with another Memorandum by the Minister of Land and Natural Resources.[150] The officials had worked quickly, their proposals having been considered by an *ad hoc* committee of Ministers on 23 September. The chief deliberation had concerned the suggested grant of concurrent powers to the Countryside Commission to provide facilities widely in the national interest when local authorities were unable or unwilling to do so. It had not been found possible to define the circumstances in which these powers might be exercised in such a way as to prevent local authorities leaving to the Commission work which they should do themselves. Accordingly the Minister dropped this particular idea. What was now proposed was a list of eight measures which required legislation:

1. The National Parks Commission should be reconstituted as The Countryside Commission.
2. County Councils should be empowered to establish Country

Parks, of a kind previously referred to as 'countryside recreation sites'. Exchequer grant would be payable.

3. Local authorities should be encouraged to provide certain camping and caravan sites, with the aid of grant.

4. Grant should be paid towards the additional administrative expenses of the National Park planning authorities.

5. Grant should be paid for the removal of eyesores, for tree planting and tree preservation, and for providing access to open country, throughout the countryside.

6. Deficiencies in powers to control traffic in National Parks should be rectified.

7. Grant should be paid towards the cost of treatment of derelict land throughout the country.

8. There should be minor amendments made to existing legislation dealing with tree preservation, footpaths, method of appointment of National Park planning authorities, provision of toilets and facilities for collecting litter, and local authorities' powers to control activities interfering with the quiet enjoyment of the countryside.

The Minister proposed to consult the local authority associations, to arrange for the drafting of a Bill, and to make a statement (rather than prepare a White Paper) about Government intentions at the Countryside in 1970 Conference to be held in November 1965. These steps were agreed, subject to further discussion with the Treasury on the payment of grants towards administrative expenses of National Park authorities, and with the Minister of Housing and Local Government on the possibility of giving further financial assistance to the most needy local authorities, over and above an Exchequer grant of 50% and the appropriate Rates Support Grant.

The die was virtually cast. The first excesses of M.L.N.R. had been curbed and the outlines of a new Bill were now sketched in a way that built on the outlook that had begun to develop in M.H.L.G. during 1964. The focus had shifted dramatically from National Parks to Country Parks. The political and financial constraints that had attended the prospects for a simple amending Bill between 1957 and 1963 were removed in an upsurge of concern for the provision of new facilities in the countryside. What was soon lost was any pretence as to a comprehensive, countryside policy; this disappeared in the discussion of responsibilities between M.L.N.R. and M.H.L.G. and did not emerge again. The proposed Bill essentially was a measure for maintaining legislation for National Parks, extending grant aid to a range of facilities within and outside National Parks, and introducing a new facility in a form to be known as country parks. The latent, emotional issues of National Park administration, central versus local control, and preservation of amenity in the national interest were conveniently put on one side.

The Minister's long awaited White Paper, *Leisure in the Countryside*[151] was published in February 1966. A new Commission, further financial assistance and a package of new proposals, some firm but others still tentative, was outlined relating to the countryside as a whole, including country parks, picnic sites, access to water and open country, footpaths and bridleways, and trees and woodlands. The purpose behind these objectives was to bring existing legislation up to date in the light of newly perceived community needs: 'developments have been more rapid, and on a greater scale, than could have been foreseen in 1949, when the country was only beginning to recover from the war. Now that there is more money, more leisure, and above all there are more cars, if the original intentions of the National Parks and Countryside Act, 1949, are to be fulfilled, and if the National Parks are to retain their distinctive character, then it is essential to make new provision for the enjoyment of the countryside elsewhere both to meet public demand and to relieve pressure on remote or outstandingly beautiful places' (paragraph 7).

This prelude to new legislation enabled Ministers in July and August that year to consider further a number of possible additions to, or changes in, the proposals outlined in the White Paper.[152] They agreed the following. The first consideration was to set up a Footpaths Committee. Progress in making the survey of footpaths and bridleways, required of County Councils under the 1949 Act, had been disappointing. The situation demanded a review of administrative and procedural matters. (Subsequently, Sir Arthur Gosling was appointed chairman of such a Committee; the *Report of the Footpaths Committee* was published in 1968.* Some of the recommendations were subsequently incorporated in the new Act. The White Paper had expressed hopes of establishing 'a carefully-planned network' of footpaths and bridleways, some based on existing routes, but others newly created. The Gosling Committee did not find favour with this idea, preferring to see the value and charm of footpaths in their 'waywardness'.)

The second idea was to invite the National Parks Commission to survey England and Wales to determine which woodlands of (say) five acres or more should be retained generally under a broad leaf crop. It was accepted that it would be unnecessary to do this if local conferences such as those proposed for the Chilterns and the Weald could be made to serve the same purpose. (In fact the point

---

* The terms of reference were: 'To consider how far the present system of footpaths, bridleways and other comparable rights of way in England and Wales and the arrangements for the recording, closure, diversion, creation and maintenance of such routes are suitable for present and potential needs in the countryside and to make recommendations.' The Committee was set up in March 1967.

of the Minister's concern was largely met, in that following the Chilterns Beechwood Conference in 1967 there were three further Conferences in 1968 in respect of the Weald, of Essex and Hertfordshire, and of Shropshire, Staffordshire and Warwickshire, when the importance of woodland management to considerations of landscape were stressed to large and representative audiences.)

Third, it was thought that the Forestry Commission should have power to acquire, plant and manage woods in the interests of amenity and public access; also to pay grant to private owners to plant and manage woods in the interests of amenity; also to pay a new grant (higher than that paid for commercial planting) for planting broad leaved trees in the interests of amenity. Fourth, a suggestion was to empower county councils to provide lavatories on holiday routes with the aid of a 75% grant where they were required to prevent damage to the countryside.

There were other small matters requiring agreement, but the preparation of the Bill could now be set in hand. Departmental restructuring meant no delay. In February 1967 the Ministry of Land and Natural Resources ended its short life and was integrated with the Ministry of Housing and Local Government; the Secretary of State for Wales remained responsible for National Parks, long distance footpaths and Areas of Outstanding Natural Beauty in Wales and Monmouthshire. It was therefore the new Ministry, now under Anthony Greenwood,* which was responsible for the Bill and for dealing with the many representations on the new provisions.

In the meantime, the dissolution of the old Ministry meant some adjustment in the advisory Sub-Committees that existed.[153] The Natural Resources Advisory Committee, previously chaired by Sir Dudley Stamp, was discontinued. The work of the Minerals Sub-Committee was adopted by a consultative Committee appointed by the Natural Environment Research Council. The Land Use Data Sub-Committee was not reappointed, but the Land Use Sub-Committee was succeeded by a new Committee appointed to advise the Minister on problems arising from the use of rural land in England and Wales for leisure and recreation. In September 1967 Professor G. P. Wibberley assumed the Chairmanship of the new Land Use (Recreation and Leisure) Committee—in many ways a symptomatic change from the previous committees, reflecting the new outlook on countryside matters.

The emphasis on a countryside policy was widely welcomed, and this deflected attention from the long-standing grievances on local amenity issues and National Parks administration. Consequently the representations over the Bill were of no great significance, there

---

* Mr. Greenwood replaced Mr. Crossman on 11 August 1966.

being little or no opposition to what was being proposed. This is not to say however that opportunities were not taken for old National Park hobby-horses to be ridden again. Indeed, they gave rise to some of the strongest comments. The Standing Committee on National Parks, for example, welcomed the principle of Joint Planning Boards in inter-county National Parks (as outlined in paragraph 13 of the 1966 White Paper) but were disappointed that there was still no firm assurance that the principle would be generally applied. They wanted adequate default powers where local authorities were unwilling to act.[154] There were also persistent individual agitators: Peter Jackson, M.P., and Lady Sayer of the Dartmoor Preservation Society to name but two. Among local authorities and other bodies Somerset County Council was prominent in its concern about ploughing and fencing of open moorland within the Exmoor National Park; and The Chiltern Society about local amenity issues. Local authorities ever conscious of the need for powers to control their own affairs, were dissatisfied with the clause whereby County District Councils could only exercise powers in relation to country parks with the consent of the County Council.* A general, widespread feeling was that 'National Parks' should be retained in the title of the new Act; there were suspicions that in fact National Parks were being devalued by the new legislation.

But it was the sharpness of Lady Sayer's criticism of the Bill that provides the main link with the 1949 Act and the amenity issues concerning National Parks. In a memo to the Minister, Greenwood, in November 1967 she wrote 'As far as Dartmoor is concerned, the Bill as at present drafted is bitterly disappointing. It appears to leave the National Park no better protected, and with no better prospect of improved administration, than at present'.[155] An accompanying note gave examples of the failures in the Dartmoor National Park administration due to County Council control and the imbalance of nationally-nominated to local authority-appointed members on the Dartmoor National Park Committee. 'Since Dartmoor was designated a National Park in 1951 the standards of its protection have steadily declined. The Service departments now train over more of Dartmoor than they did then—an additional training area at Burrator has been added without a public enquiry, and exercises take place outside the specified training areas—and with more damaging effect; the spread and dereliction of industrial activity has increased, building standards have declined; more beautiful woodlands have been destroyed; more conifer-planting

---

* The Ministry considered that it made for better administration if the primary responsibility for country parks lay with the County Councils. The Secretary of State met representatives of the Rural District Councils Association in October 1967 when he stressed then (and later, during the Second Reading) that District Councils had the right of appeal against a refusal of consent by a County Council.

has invaded open moorland; more prehistoric and historic remains have been obliterated or destroyed; a giant television mast now dominates central Dartmoor; the upper Avon valley has been submerged; more disfiguring electricity poles have been allowed; more wild country has been ploughed and access lost; and many more motor vehicles now trespass over Dartmoor's moorland tracks and commons.'

The articulate, ardent fervour of the amenity propagandists had not been lost. The new enthusiasm for country parks and other countryside measures could not extinguish the old flame of concern. There was still the touching faith in 'proper' administration of Park areas. The determination to see the control of development in terms of right or wrong according to fixed amenity criteria allowed no half measures, and both Central Government and local authorities came under attack for their 'weaknesses'. In these senses the position had not changed from 1949, but on 3 July 1968 the Countryside Act received the Royal Assent and the National Parks story entered a new phase.

CHAPTER 8

Legislation for Scotland

THE twenty years between 1948 and 1968 in relation to development in Scotland can be divided into three very distinct and separate periods. The first lasted until 1960 when the Scottish Office, in spite of the Ramsay Committee Reports, was lukewarm to the idea of a National Parks Act on English lines. The very different Scottish situation was apparent to many and no moves were made to emulate English developments. The second extended from 1960 to 1964 when two separate Bills foundered. There was no mention of National Parks, but they sought to extend the scale of grant aid for amenity purposes in the countryside; the second was particularly concerned with tourism. The period 1965–67 marked the formative years when the Countryside in 1970 Conference promoted a new look at countryside policy and advocated the new facility of country parks. A Scottish Countryside Act in 1967 was on very similar lines to the English Countryside Act, 1968.

No National Parks Act for Scotland

With the submission of the Ramsay Report in 1947 the immediate indications were that a National Parks Bill for Scotland would be introduced. But feeling against this course of action soon hardened. There was an abundance of Commissions and Committees and the Department of Health for Scotland (then the responsible Ministry for planning in Scotland) considered that now the National Park areas had been chosen, preliminary planning work could be undertaken in conjunction with the local authorities. An advisory committee was as much as was required.

It was known that there were some initial Ministerial reservations in England about the advisability of setting up a new body (see page 82), although because of general expectations, a Commission would in fact be established. It was thought, however, that the position in Scotland with regard to National Parks differed considerably from England and Wales, and that the reservations about a Commission could be very much stronger. The factors were as follows:

a. The problem in England was one of protection, conservation, and opening for public use. In Scotland, it was more a problem of rehabilitation and development* of the areas concerned by the encouragement of tourism and rural industries. There was a fundamentally different approach to the problem in the two countries.

b. In England, the Hobhouse proposals meant that the National Park Committees very largely usurped the planning functions of the local planning authority. The Scottish recommendations were that the Parks Planning Committee should be a Committee of the local planning authority with one-third representation nominated by the National Parks Commission. (In practice, the English solution in single County National Parks was to accept this organisational device.)

c. No conservation areas were proposed for Scotland.

d. There was the great problem of finance required to carry out the development and administration of the Parks. Local bodies could not undertake this themselves. Resources were slender in the Highland Counties.

e. The Scottish Committee had not dealt with the general question of access to the countryside, because of differences in land law from England.

f. The Scottish Committee had envisaged a somewhat greater measure of collaboration between the Scottish National Parks Commission and agencies such as the Forestry Commission.

g. In Scotland there was more emphasis on the acquisition of land. For many the spectre of land nationalisation was a crucial determinant.

The Secretary of State, A. Woodburn, reported these views to the Lord President's Committee in April 1948.[156] In his Memorandum he said that he had not yet had an opportunity of discussing the recommendations of the Ramsay Report (Cmd. 7235) with the local authorities and other bodies concerned and had not reached any considered views as to the lines which Scottish legislation should take. He did not regard the need for such legislation 'as one of pressing urgency' and would be content if the legislation were deferred until the 1949–50 Session, or until the next Parliament. This approach contrasts markedly with the developments already put under way by Silkin for National Parks in England.

But if the Secretary of State showed little enthusiasm, other bodies did. That same month* at the first meeting of the Scottish Economic Conference, it was agreed that the Department of Health should call together the various interests concerned to report on progress which might be made towards the establishment of National Parks.[157] Pressure came from another source too. The Scottish Council for National Parks wrote to the Secretary of State in June

---

* 23 April 1948.

pressing for National Parks and an indication as to when legislation was likely to be introduced.

A further meeting of the Scottish Economic Conference, held in July 1948, was attended by representatives of: Aberdeen, Argyll, Banff, Dumbarton, Inverness, Perth, Stirling and Ross and Cromarty Councils; the Forestry Commission, the Scottish Tourist Board, British Transport Commission, Ministry of Transport, North of Scotland Hydro Electric Board, the Scottish Home Department, Department of Agriculture, Education Department and the Department of Health. A Working Party under the chairmanship of an official of the Department of Health was set up to consider how far existing powers could be used, pending the passing of National Parks legislation, to further the purposes which the Scottish National Parks Committee had had in mind, and to work out schemes for the proposed National Park areas.

Schemes could not be prepared for all areas immediately because of the dearth of survey information. But there could be work on the Loch Lomond-Trossachs area, and this Report was submitted to the Secretary of State in December 1949. Prominence was given to the provision and regulation of access, holiday accommodation and recreational facilities. This was not a comprehensive plan for a National Park, but it indicated what could be done under the powers that then existed.[158]

By this time the English National Parks Bill had passed through Parliament. There was still an understanding that a Scottish Bill would follow, but no time was set. In fact, two years of very little activity on this front was positive rather than negative: no decision to legislate implied a decision not to legislate. The difficulties confirmed the grounds for caution.[159] The English Act placed the responsibility for the planning of National Parks on local bodies. But the lack of resources in Scottish counties for the task of running and developing the Parks suggested that a scheme to follow the English pattern would be ineffective in Scotland. The only feasible alternative was some form of central administration with executive functions and wholly financed by the Exchequer. But the likelihood of Treasury support was minimal, particularly in view of the fact that even greater expenditure would be needed for Scottish Parks because so far they were relatively undeveloped. Furthermore, it could not be shown that there were acute problems of preservation and access. Above all, Scottish National Parks called for development rather than protection; but the Highland local planning authorities had neither the staff, the resources nor the will to develop. As a consequence, the lobby for National Parks was outweighed by the strong vested interests ranged in opposition to the Parks. They could rehearse an argument long familiar in England, although it

143

served to retard rather than promote the provision of Parks. They argued that facilities and aspects of development such as roads should not be provided in National Parks when they were not being provided for the local population in the remainder of the authority's area; and that as Scottish National Parks were essentially national assets, they should be paid for nationally.

In these circumstances it was maintained that it was convenient to postpone a Scottish Bill until English experience had been gained. The Legislation Committee asked the Scottish Office to consider a Bill if one were to be required, but in February 1950 it was decided to prepare no Bill at the present time. Meanwhile the Secretary of State had the advantage of a 'safety net' in respect of the five National Park areas. Article 5 of the Town and Country Planning (General Development) (Scotland) Order, 1948, required County Councils to furnish him particulars of every application for permission to carry out development in the parts of their districts lying within the proposed National Parks. Furthermore, it could always be shown that promotional work was continuing. The Working Party of the Scottish Economic Conference proceeded with its surveys of the five areas. The Forestry Commission already had its National Forest Parks, and the Nature Conservancy established a National Nature Reserve in Wester Ross and the Cairngorms.

With the lapse of time, however, it seemed that if legislation could be decently postponed further, it should be so. A change of Government in 1951 held out no new prospects. The Scottish Council for National Parks (Chairman, Lord Keith) still urging a Commission, held a meeting with Lord Home, Minister of State, in June 1952, but the difficulties of finance and a congested legislative programme were now held to override the general acceptance of the principle of National Parks.[160] With no likelihood of official encouragement, enthusiasm for National Parks waned, and a distinct period seemed to come to an end.

The matter fell into abeyance for a number of years. Throughout the fifties there was simply no political will for a National Parks Bill, and the amenity bodies were nowhere near as firmly entrenched as in England. Above all, the Highland planning authorities were strongly in favour of maintaining the *status quo*: they had neither staff, resources nor inclination to engage in National Park planning. They were not innovative authorities and indeed, it was not until the 1960s that the majority of these counties even began to submit their required Development Plans. With deadlock in England and Wales over any amendment to the 1949 Act the National Parks issue in Scotland lay virtually dormant. Occasional flurries of interest roused speculation, but they were of little consequence. In 1955 Dunbarton County Council expressed interest in a Loch

Lomond/Trossachs National Park. In that year also, and in 1959, the District Councils Association passed a resolution, based on one by the Badenoch District Council of Inverness-shire, urging National Parks for Scotland, particularly a Cairngorm Park.[161]

Abortive Bills, 1960–64

New Government initiative came with a proposal of the Secretary of State, J. Maclay, for a scheme for Exchequer grants to be made available towards the cost of projects designed to conserve or enhance rural amenities in Scotland. His ideas were contained in a Memorandum 'Preservation of the Countryside'[162] considered by Home Affairs Committee on 19 July 1960.[163] He suggested that there were two ways of dealing with areas of special amenity in Scotland. One, favoured by the Scottish Council for National Parks, supported the establishment of a National Parks authority and the formal designation of National Parks areas on the English model. Another, favoured by the National Trust, argued that the greater part of the Highlands and much of the Lowlands had high amenity value and that what was required was a flexible scheme for channelling Exchequer money into specific prospects for the improvement or preservation of amenity by voluntary bodies, local authorities and landowners. The National Trust advocated an advisory Council for Places of National Beauty to advise the Secretary of State.

He favoured this proposal, considering it analogous to the arrangements under which the Historic Buildings Council for Scotland advised the Minister of Works and the Secretary of State. He thought that the measures that might be assisted could include the signposting of rights of way, provision of lay-bys at scenic vantage points on private roads to which the landowner had given access, and 'face lifting' in villages. He proposed a total annual allotment of not more than £10,000. The Committee approved the proposal and the Home Secretary authorised the preparation of a Bill for submission to the Legislation Committee. The origins behind this new proposal are obscure but the weight attached to the National Trust's own ideas suggests their influence. Certainly this was a period when the Trust's face lift schemes had widespread support.

A draft Countryside (Scotland) Bill was prepared for the Legislation Committee in April 1961.[164] A small measure of eleven clauses, it was designed to give effect to the proposals approved by the Home Affairs Committee the previous July. The primary purpose was to enable Exchequer grants to be paid, on the recommendation of a Scottish Countryside Council, to local authorities, voluntary organisations and individual persons towards the cost of minor works which preserved or enhanced the natural beauty of Scotland. It was estimated that expenditure would rise to £25,000 per year when the scheme was under way. The Bill also filled in a few minor gaps in the existing statutory powers of local authorities; these related to litter bins and the collection of litter.

Consultations with outside interests had shown that these additional powers and the grant scheme would be generally welcomed. The Secretary of State's Memorandum for the Committee declared that 'The Bill will not be controversial—it is supported by the National Trust for Scotland and other representative amenity bodies and its principles are accepted by the Scottish local authority associations'.

In discussion it was considered that the scheme for grants was generous and flexible—more so than in comparable English legislation, and it was asked whether this might cause some embarrassment to the Minister of Housing, especially as grants could be made direct to private persons. Another point of concern was clause 8 in the Bill which provided that any agreement made between a local authority and a private landowner for the provision of facilities to the public on private land, and for access thereto, could be enforced against successors in title. Was it certain that organisations representing Scottish landowners had no objection to these additional powers? But subject to further consideration of these matters, and provided that the scheme be reviewed every two to three years, Legislation Committee approved the draft Bill and authorised its introduction on a date to be agreed.

But it became clear that the proposals were unpopular with the Association of County Councils. The Councils preferred to deal direct with the Secretary of State and to get their grants direct from him. They feared the role of the Advisory Council as a high powered amenity lobby. Another weighty obstacle was the lack of Parliamentary time, and the Bill was not proceeded with.

Mr. Maclay's successor as Secretary of State, M. Noble, followed with a Countryside and Tourist Amenities (Scotland) Bill two years later, proposals being approved by Home Affairs Committee at their meeting on 28 June 1963.[165] The new concern was tourism. In June 1962 local authorities were asked by Circular* to survey their areas with two objectives: the definition of areas of great landscape value and the preparation and submission of tourist development proposals. When complete they would enable the Department to form a comprehensive national scheme for the preservation of the countryside and the development of tourism. A measure of the local authority response can be gathered by the fact that by January 1963 30 out of 31 counties and 23 out of 26 Burghs had given interim replies; no plans had been received.[166]

---

* SDD2/1962. (The Scottish Development Department was now the responsible Ministry for planning.)

But the National Parks issue, English style, was not dead either. In 1963 Lord Silkin was in contact with Lord Craigton, Minister of State at the Scottish Office: Silkin had in mind that a Scottish Peer might institute a Lords debate on the extension of National Parks in Scotland. Craigton avoided the debate, doubting whether any advantage would be gained from designating National Parks in Scotland.[167]

The new Bill resurrected the provisions of the 1961 Bill and added clauses to establish a Scottish Tourist Fund, financed by a levy from the Scottish hotel industry. Safely passing the Home Affairs Committee, it was approved by Legislation Committee on 8 October 1963. A Scottish Tourist Amenities Council was proposed to advise the Secretary of State on the payment of grants for amenity work (as proposed in the earlier Bill) and to administer the Scottish Tourist Fund. It gave powers to local authorities to preserve and enhance the natural beauty of the countryside, to bring into use derelict or unsightly land, to provide litter bins and remove litter, and to advertise the amenities of the area. The Amenities Council would also make grants or loans from the Tourist Fund for the provision, maintenance or improvement of tourist facilities in Scotland. The Fund would be financed by a levy on the hotel industry. It was made clear that no grants or loans could be given for the provision, maintenance or improvement of hotels and boarding houses which provided accommodation for profit.

The Fund had been proposed by the Scottish Tourist Board in April 1962 after discussions with the Scottish Committees of the hoteliers organisations.[168] There seemed to be no practical alternative to contributions from the industry; leading hoteliers agreed, and Scottish Members of Parliament on both sides of the House had also come to this view. But the provisions in the Bill were strongly attacked by the British Hotels and Restaurants Association and the British Travel and Holidays Association. This led the Scottish Tourist Board to consider after all that the fund must be financed in some other way—although it was apparent that the fund could not be financed from the Exchequer or from local rates.

The other proposal, for an Amenities Council to receive an Exchequer grant, also (and again) ran into difficulties. Contention was aroused between the amenity societies and the local authorities on the powers to be given to the new Council. The local authorities were increasingly opposed to anybody coming between them and the Secretary of State. They were very suspicious of the proposal of the National Trust for Scotland to enlarge the Amenity Council's functions to include an overall power to advise on and supervise all developments affecting amenity.

With these problems, the Secretary of State was left with little option but to abandon the Bill. In his Memorandum to Committee in February 1964[169] he recommended that Government should not proceed with the Bill. Not all was lost however: the Bill's minor provisions which extended local authorities' powers to carry out amenity work were added to the Local Government (Development and Finance) (Scotland) Bill which had already been introduced.

So the Conservative Administration which inherited the National Parks legislation in 1951 had by 1964, when it left office, failed to introduce amending legislation for England and Wales and had made little progress in Scotland. National Parks for Scotland were never seriously contemplated in official circles but at least the Countryside and Tourism Bill would have empowered the Secretary of State to make grants calculated to preserve or enhance the natural beauty of the countryside or to improve facilities available to the public for its enjoyment—similar to grants already available in England and Wales within National Park areas. With these and other powers Scotland would have achieved the same general objective as the 1949 Act, though without the Commission and the Park designation procedure.

The Countryside (Scotland) Act, 1967

The matter of the Tourist Fund and the Amenities Council proved to be a cul-de-sac in the Scottish story. When countryside questions were raised again it was on lines parallel to the proposals of the Minister of Land and Natural Resources in 1965 in respect of England and Wales. As we saw in Chapter 7 (page 134) Willey's first ideas were considered at Home Affairs Committee in July 1965. So far there had been no Scottish move, but it was clear that the Scottish Office would have to do something. At the General Election the Labour Party was committed to a review of legislation. Their manifesto *Signposts for Scotland* had read:

> 'At present Scotland has no counterpart to the National Parks Commission south of the Border. Labour intends greatly to extend the power of the National Parks Commission for England and Wales and to make it the chief agency for the use of public funds for preserving and promoting enjoyment of the beauty of the countryside. It will function in much the same way as the Arts Council and the Sports Council of Great Britain which a Labour Government is also pledged to set up. Scotland must have a comparable authority.'

This encouraged the Scottish Council for National Parks to keep up their pressure. On 4 February 1965 a delegation from the Council was received by Lord Hughes, an Under-Secretary of State at the Scottish Office. Some months later (27 May) they forwarded a lengthy memorandum recommending National Parks for Scotland and control of the countryside in Scotland under an Act for the whole country.[170]

But as 16 years before, Scottish circumstances were significantly different from those in England and Wales. Moreover, in recent years there had been certain developments which had reinforced the differences. For example, in the Highlands (where four out of five likely National Parks were located) the Highlands and Islands Development Board, set up in 1965, had adequate executive powers which could be used for recreation provision. Second, the recently reconstituted Scottish Tourist Board was likely to concern itself with countryside matters, including camping and caravans. Thirdly, the Forestry Commission was an active agency, and had declared their concern to provide access and recreation facilities. Fourth, it had to be admitted that planning control by the local planning authorities in the designated National Park areas had worked well. Moreover, their plans under Circular 2/1962 (see page 146) could provide a basis for grants towards development work. The local authorities also had new powers to preserve or enhance land amenities and to provide facilities for public enjoyment of the countryside, by virtue of the Local Government (Development and Finance) (Scotland) Act, 1964. Fifth, if a central technical advisory service were needed the Scottish Development Department was likely to be able to do all that a Commission could do.

In the late 1940s and early 1950s the distinctiveness of the Scottish situation was sufficiently pronounced for National Parks legislation to be resisted. But the tide was now running strongly in favour of a Countryside Commission, and in the event this particular enthusiasm proved too strong for any other alternative. In England, the Minister for Land and Natural Resources was determined to follow this course of action, and Scotland would have been put in an invidious position if they had not followed suit. The clinching factor was the speculation aroused by the Countryside in 1970 Conference. A Scottish Study Group under the chairmanship of Professor Robert Grieve, asked to consider Scottish countryside problems in preparation for the Conference in November 1965, was understood to be likely to recommend a Commission with executive powers working in parallel with local planning authorities. (In fact the Grieve Report[171] recommended: the establishment of a Countryside Commission in Scotland as a central agency to determine countryside standards and policy, to recommend grant to other authorities and to carry out with its own executive arm those projects which cannot be handled by existing agencies.)

It will be recalled that after the Home Affairs Committee in July 1965, an Interdepartmental Working Party of Officials was constituted to work out detailed proposals. The Minister of Land and Natural Resources put his revised proposals to the Home Affairs Committee in October. He said he would make known his proposals to the Countryside in 1970 Conference in November. At this meeting the Secretary of State for Scotland, W. Ross, also announced his intention to establish a Commission. He was clearly influenced by the Grieve Report for he specifically reserved his position on the question of executive powers for the Commission: he said he might want to come forward later with proposals for a Scottish Commission which differed from the English proposals. The Scottish statement was given in reply to a Parliamentary Question on 17 November. Once more England and Scotland were back in step.

The Secretary of State announced in principle the establishment of a Scottish Countryside Commission. The detailed functions would suit Scotland's distinctive needs. It would be co-ordinated with the work of existing agencies, local authorities and voluntary bodies: 'It is the Government's intention to establish a Countryside Commission for Scotland, and to ensure that such a Commission and the Scottish local authorities will have all the powers necessary not only to conserve our unique heritage of scenic beauty but to see that its recreational and tourist potential is developed to the full. Our proposals will be framed to suit Scotland's distinctive needs, and will provide for appropriate Exchequer assistance. The new machinery will supplement and fit in not only with Government agencies such as the Highlands and Islands Development Board, the Forestry Commission and the Nature Conservancy but also with the existing structure of local authorities and voluntary bodies.'

Much remained for discussion and clarification for little preparatory work had been undertaken so far. Consultations were set in hand with a large number of bodies. Most broadly welcomed the proposal, but significant reservation came from the Association of County Councils in Scotland. At a meeting with the Minister of State, G. Willis, on 18 February 1966 they made it clear that the Association believed that a Scottish Countryside Commission was unnecessary. Their argument was a familiar one: the purposes of the Commission could best be left to local planning authorities in the exercise of their statutory powers and to the Secretary of State as the final arbiter in planning matters.

The Secretary of State prepared a Memorandum, 'Policy for the Scottish Countryside',[172] for Home Affairs Committee in October 1966,[173] following his discussions with the various interested bodies. He raised four main issues. First, the powers of the Countryside Commission: in view of the fact that rural councils were relatively small, financially constricted and inadequately staffed, their efforts had to be supplemented by those of a Commission 'equipped with sufficient executive powers to enable it to make its own direct contribution to the solution of countryside problems'. He made it clear that the Commission should not be, nor be allowed to develop into, the main executive agency for carrying out projects to improve and develop the countryside, and it was therefore necessary to define the circumstances in which the Commission's executive powers could be exercised: he suggested that the Commission should carry out only 'prototype' developments. Other powers would be the undertaking of research and provision of an information service. The Secretary of State favoured the idea of the Commission setting up local machinery to deal with areas of national importance by working in fuller co-operation with the local authorities concerned. But in discussion it was the proposed executive power to undertake prototype developments that commanded attention. The point was made that the power would probably be used for relatively minor projects such as the study which the Highlands and Islands Development Board was carrying out in Glencoe on a caravan site. The Committee agreed in principle but the discussion implied a much reduced scale of direct executive action from what originally had been in mind.

Second, with regard to planning control, the Secretary of State made it clear that he did not wish to interpose the Commission in the statutory planning machinery between the local planning authorities and himself. The Commission's function would be to assist the authorities and to act in association with the control of countryside developments. This was vague, but had been generally accepted by those consulted, including the County Councils Association.

Third, the Secretary of State proposed that the Scottish authorities should be given a number of miscellaneous powers, already available to English local authorities under the 1949 Act.

Fourth, on finance, the Secretary of State reminded his colleagues that the Cabinet had already agreed that the 75% grant towards current expenditure and loan charges should apply to Scotland.[174] But he added that it would be necessary for the Commission to be able to make once and for all grants and loans in suitable circumstances to assist voluntary bodies or private persons to undertake important recreational projects which local authorities were unable to do; and to undertake the executive work mentioned above. He thought that expenditure over three years after the passing of the Bill might be as follows:

	£ 1st Year	£ 2nd Year	£ 3rd Year
1. Countryside Commission (admin. and other overheads including information and research)	50,000	100,000	150,000
2. Commission schemes	50,000	50,000	50,000
3. 75% grants to local authorities	50,000	100,000	200,000
	150,000	250,000	400,000

151

There is little further of significance to record. The Countryside (Scotland) Bill was accompanied by an Explanatory and Financial Memorandum (there was no White Paper as with England and Wales). Part I of the Bill dealt with the establishment and powers of the Commission. Clause 5 related to the 'prototype developments' previously advocated by the Secretary of State: this term was lost but the Commission were enabled to submit proposals for development projects or schemes which involved the application of 'new and developed methods, concepts or techniques' or which illustrated the appropriateness of projects to other areas which presented similar problems. In fact, although the actual wording was slightly different, this was followed in the English legislation a year later. A common approach was maintained in spite of the Secretary of State's earlier desire to give his Commission a wider executive function than for England and Wales. Part II dealt with access to open country; Part III with public paths and long distance routes. In Part IV provision was made for the creation of country parks, and further powers were conferred on local authorities for the development of facilities and other arrangements. And so, apart from the designation of National Parks, Scotland was now to be on a very similar basis to England and Wales. The Act reached the Statute Book on 27 October 1967, nine months ahead of the English legislation.

CHAPTER 9

Conclusions and Overview

read this particularly

IN July 1971 a Government Committee was set up under the chairmanship of Lord Sandford 'to review how far the National Parks have fulfilled the purposes for which they were established; to consider the implications of the changes that have occurred, and may be expected, in social and economic conditions; and to make recommendations as regards future policies'. The Report of Lord Sandford's Committee was published in April 1974.[175] It contained ample proof of the fact that the Countryside Act, 1968, in no way marked an end to the high feelings which have been generated about National Park planning. The issues it reviewed were familiar ones. For example, the reconciliation of the preservation and enhancement of beauty with the promotion of public enjoyment; the conflict between amenity values and compelling national necessities; and the question of park administration, all appear as longstanding problems over a period of 20 years or more.

On the other hand it is fair to say that the situation has recently changed, largely as a result of local government reorganisation. There has been a radical recasting of the National Park authorities, with seven of them now committees of a single county council. The Peak and the Lake District remain planning boards, with the power to settle their own finances by precepting on the rates of their constituent authorities. National Park Planning Officers with full time staffs have been appointed with responsibilities of preparing National Park plans, under the Local Government Act, 1972. Additionally, the Local Government Finance Act, 1974, introduced a supplementary block grant for National Parks, and in spite of reservations as to just how much money National Parks will actually receive, none the less the financial situation has improved.

In spite of these very recent events, some of the fundamental difficulties about National Parks and access to the countryside remain as before. This volume on the contemporary history of Land Use and Environmental Planning is by no means self-contained; its main themes have not yet been worked out. In bringing together, therefore, in this summary chapter the important conclusions from the National Parks story to 1968, we should bear in mind that we are in fact reviewing an on-going saga.

F

National Parks fall readily into the evolutionary pattern of British land use planning. Their history shows features which have obvious similarity to the development of other aspects of planning. There were, for example, three phases, the recognition of which can be applied to other branches of planning history.

The first was in the 1930s when the problems which we recognise today were first being perceived and defined. At that time, cautious legislation dealt with the more pressing issues, without in any way getting to the heart of the matter. The idea of National Parks had been examined by the Addison Committee, without result, and it was left to the Standing Conference on National Parks to become their chief advocates. But land development pressures were not likely to cause serious landscape damage at least in the short term, and for some years the chief focus of public disquiet was not National Parks but access to open country. Town planning schemes prepared under the Town and Country Planning Act, 1932, could allocate land for open space; restrictive residential density provisions could attempt to preserve large-scale countryside areas; voluntary agreements could reserve smaller amenity areas; and around London at least there could be some action towards a green belt, but the net result of these provisions was an inconclusive and unconvincing land use policy. In the meantime there was in the grouse moors of the north, a sharp conflict with sporting rights which made prominent the issue of public use of private land for mass recreation purposes. The outdoor amenity bodies had a new-found importance at a time when there was popular interest in physical recreation and outdoor activities such as cycling, hosteling, camping and rambling. A legislative response was the Access to Mountains Act, 1939, although it proved abortive in practice.

The second phase covered the whole of the 1940s when the question of National Parks grew in significance during the wartime reconstruction period and the immediate post-war years. Legislation gave sweeping new powers in relation to the problems which first arose in the 1930s but which were sharply articulated in the 1940s. It was a case of Government reacting to a popular demand, which caught the imagination of many and incurred the hostility of very few, ably fanned by powerful interest groups. During the war years the promise of National Parks was an easy and acceptable offering as part of the new Britain to be built after the war was over. They seemed to be demanding neither in legislative nor in their financial implications. They also complemented other aspects of land use planning in the context of greater central initiatives than had hitherto been the case in the British experience. By 1945 successive Ministers and other Government spokesmen had expressed themselves in favour of National Parks and it would have been surprising if any immediate post-war Government had not taken some action to implement a National Parks policy. In the event, the Dower Report of 1945 and the Hobhouse Report of 1947 ensured success for the National Parks movement in England and Wales (although in Scotland the Ramsay Reports did not have this outcome).

The third phase is the remaining period, the 1950s onwards, when we have evidence of the actual operation of the 1949 Act. In fact, difficulties abounded over a number of issues: the rigidity of interpreting the need to preserve amenity against other development pressures; the role of the National Parks Commission, buffeted between the Ministry of Housing and Local Government on the one hand and the amenity bodies on the other; the lack of money for National Park purposes; the poor spending rate of many Park authorities; and the wounding disputes as to central versus local control in Park administration. Attempts to revise legislation were not successful and, finally, the Countryside Acts, 1967, and 1968 gave powers to deal with new land use and environmental problems in terms of meeting recreation needs in areas outside the National Parks and nearer to the major centres of urban population.

These three phases accord closely with other aspects of planning over the last 30 years and provide a useful framework for considering the broad course of developments in land use planning. The key years were the wartime period when the basis of a centralist planning system was laid. A measure of co-ordinated central control was attempted over land use, development, strategic growth, population and employment distribution, and investment and social policy. The reasons for this intense political activity and speculation were related to a blend of circumstances peculiar to the war years: central co-ordination in economic and manpower planning had been successfully achieved, albeit of necessity, and there was a determination that Britain could realistically build for the future through reliance on central interventionist programmes. A policy for the countryside was an obvious component of this flurry of innovation.

What followed this watershed period can be regarded as the working out in practice of the land use planning system decided upon and the measures provided to sustain it. The period 1945–52 provided the cornerstones of post-war land use planning: the Distribution of Industry Act, 1945, the New Towns Act, 1946, the Town and Country Planning Act, 1947, the National Parks and Access to the Countryside Act, 1949, and the Town Development Act, 1952. The framework was for control over land use and strategic development concerned with the location of work place, residence, and recreation area. It was in this package that policies for National Parks and the countryside were framed. This was the first comprehensive national land use policy to be devised, and with hindsight it gives the impression of being remarkably simple. There was certainly political and professional confidence in its achievement. But the last 20 to 25 years have made it clear that an interventionist role by Government on this scale is far from simple, and the end product may be far removed from original objectives. The lessons learned from the National Parks story are mirrored in the other related aspects of post-war planning: objectives have to be continually reassessed in the light of changing circumstances; the split between central and local government responsibilities and initiatives lead at best to an uncertain prosecution of co-ordinated policy; and in a pluralist society one set of common objectives break down before disparate interests. Post-war planning had had to be an adaptive and flexible operation.

Post-war planning got off to a remarkably confident start, and this is shared by events concerning National Parks. There was grand talk about land use planning, but few understood how it would actually work. Similarly, there was lofty speculation about the place of National Parks in post-war Britain, but naivety about their actual administration. All the formative thinking, even the deliberations of the Hobhouse Committee, took place before the new Development Plan system under the 1947 Act had come into operation, and before the division of planning responsibilities between the new planning authorities and Central Government had taken place. Even the Ministry of Town and Country Planning was a new Department, whose Minister had no Cabinet rank. In these circumstances the National Park interest groups expected and sought a form of administration for National Parks largely outside the new system. On the other hand, from the start, the Minister had to give maximum support to the system of his own creation. Herein lay seeds of difficulty. But land use planning as a control mechanism worked far better perhaps than might have been anticipated; over certain matters local authorities could be very strong, and the longer time went on there was less and less cause to fear that local authorities could not reasonably safeguard the Park areas they had to administer. Some local authorities may have been weak as innovators in country-side policy, but experience has suggested that they have been as effective as any body or agency could have been, caught up as they were in the minutiae of development control.

This brings us to the point of the role of the *ad hoc* Commission, on which so many hopes were pinned. With the uncertainties over the actual operation of post-war land use planning, and with the painful experience of the inadequate policies of the inter-war years in mind, the natural reliance of the National Park interest groups was on a Central Commission. No one knew what powers would be given by new legislation; everyone could reasonably doubt the long term constancy and ability of either central or local government to implement National Park policies. To vest power and responsibilities in a Central Commission seemed the only sure way of securing a continuous National Parks programme. In one sense it could be argued that an advisory body at least was necessary. In a difficult field where the enhancement and protection of amenity was concerned, a committee to advise on amenity questions would at least have been a wise innovation. But in 1949 the necessity for a National Parks Commission was at best debatable. The Department was always lukewarm, and at first the Minister was unconvinced. In the end a compromise arrangement resulted with functions and responsibilities split between the Commission and central and local government.

We might properly reflect on what might have happened had things turned out differently: had there been no Commission, had there been no 1949 Act, or had National Parks and countryside planning been absorbed within the normal operation of land use planning. The setting up of the Commission gave a certainty to the establishment of National Parks; charged with their designation, this at least it proceeded to do. Ten Parks had been designated by 1957 and it is questionable whether the Ministry or local authorities would have proceeded with quite that speed. It is at least possible to doubt whether the same urgency, drive or motivation would have extended to any other body but the Commission. Moreover, the existence of the Commission provided a rallying point for National Park interests and enabled amenity considerations to be brought to the Department in a way which might not otherwise have been the case. In hypothesising in this way it is not possible to argue the case in the light of Scotland which never had a National Parks Commission: there the situation was sufficiently different so that amenity interests were not deflected and the future of areas of landscape beauty was not prejudiced as might have been expected.

On the other hand, the Commission, established with fairly specific terms of reference and occupying a somewhat difficult role between conflicting interests, found it necessary to adopt a defensive position. It is true that they had certain obligations, powers and responsibilities and this made them a positive force. But the effect was that the future of National Parks, and indeed of countryside planning, became in large measure a question of whether and how far the Commission was being successful in its performance. There was therefore a degree of inflexibility about National Park planning throughout the fifties and well into the sixties. There was a rigidity of view about what needed to be done and how to go about it because of the inflexibility of the institutional framework, in particular the sensitive and delicate position of the Commission, around whom inescapably, much revolved. Adaptive policy innovations could not easily be made without compromising the constitutional position of the Commission, and in the circumstances it might be easier to do nothing.

It could always be argued that areas of fine landscape could be preserved and their amenities enhanced without the formalities of a designation process and without the intermediate role of the Commission. Responsibility for the designation of non-statutory green belts was taken by local authorities as part of their land use planning. On the other hand, with the formalities went the all important financial provisions, and in the Peak District particularly, this is where National Park planning became meaningful. From this point of view, the provisions of the 1949 Act were all-important.

On balance, therefore, the real importance of the 1949 Act was that it articulated a popular need in that it realised the hopes and aspirations of many years' active and sustained lobby by amenity interest groups. The time had come for these to be met, and not to have legislated in this way would have been to court political unpopularity. The Act provided new powers, made available financial support and created the administrative device of the Commission. But the powers were limited, for many years grant aid was very small, and the Commission ultimately had to be replaced. Here lies the crux of the matter: essentially the Act was a sop to political pressure and while the cause of National Parks themselves was protected and indeed enhanced, it can be argued that the proper development of a comprehensive countryside policy embracing National Parks and other country areas was significantly retarded. The situation was that other aspects of land use and environmental planning were essentially urban orientated, while as far as rural areas were concerned, energies and interests were for long captured by the single issue of National Parks. Developments in connection with long-distance footpaths and areas of outstanding natural beauty do not significantly weaken this argument. It was only with the countryside arguments of the sixties that anything like a comprehensive countryside policy began to emerge. It may be argued therefore that the net effect of the provisions of the 1949 Act, while meeting an important need at the time and certainly furthering National Park interests *per se*, did not significantly lead to any protection or enhancement of areas of fine landscape additional to that which might have occurred anyway through the Development Plan system. Furthermore the provisions may have prejudiced the timely emergence of effective countryside recreation planning, within which National Parks were one, but not an overriding element.

Influences on the Course of Development

There are two important points to bring out from the history of National Parks. One relates to the fact that in preparing both the 1949 Act and the 1967 and 1968 Acts Government was reacting to certain external situations. Pressure for legislation was almost entirely one way and it was largely a case of Ministers acting on external pressure, and subsequently balancing the positions of affected interest groups in proposed legislation. Government was rarely the innovator in National Parks and countryside planning; it was much more the respondent to outside recommendations. The second relates to the influences of personalities and Departments within Government on the course of events during the 30 year period. There are some important figures who played considerable roles, without whom the pattern of developments would simply not have been the same.

On the first point we have noted that the provisions of National Parks legislation were made primarily in the context of fervour for post-war reconstruction. The Addison Report of 1931 had been shelved and the 1939 Act had concerned simply access to countryside, not National Parks. But the pressure of the amenity bodies in the late 1930s found vigorous popular expression in the early 1940s: a determination to physically, and morally, renew war-torn Britain readily embraced the strong desire to protect and enhance our areas of landscape beauty and to make them freely available to the whole community. In the heady atmosphere of this period it was not practical politics to resist the promise of National Parks.

The strength of external influences on the course of events continued right throughout the period of this History. The Standing Committee on National Parks under Lord Birkett in the 1940s was of great significance. In Scotland comparable amenity interests were much weaker and this must account at least in part for the fact that a Scottish National Parks Act never materialised. In the 1960s it was the Countryside in 1970 Conference that provided the essential new material for a new approach to amending legislation. In Scotland the contribution of Professor Robert Grieve in that context was particularly influential at this time.

The transfer of interest from National Parks to country parks during the 1960s was relatively rapid. In both England and Wales and Scotland the country park idea was taken up so avidly that one is led to think that in Government circles at least it was almost a reaction to the years of failure to achieve any worthwhile amending legislation. Certain national circumstances were changing rapidly, and these provided a new set of external influences. There were three factors at least that prompted a good deal of rethinking. First, American research into the use of leisure time suggested an explosion of demand for family based, car oriented, countryside activities and there seemed no reason to suppose that this country would not follow suit. Secondly, in Britain the threat of rapidly increasing car owner-ship was now added to the expectancy of a substantial growth in population by the end of the century; a twin situation that made it more and more imperative to reconsider many land use policies, including those which had a bearing on outdoor recreation. Thirdly, greater public funds became available and the possibilities of a new scale of public investment to meet recreation demands became apparent. In 1959, Blenkinsop's Bill had foundered over Treasury resistance to meet an annual increase of grant of £40,000. Eight years later, the expected budget under the Countryside Bill was of the order of £2 millions.

With regard to the influence of personalities, Lewis Silkin stands out in his contribution. Ideologically committed to National Parks he was pragmatic enough not to be carried away by the extravagant demands of the amenity bodies. As architect of the Development Plan system for his new local planning authorities he recognised the importance of not introducing any complicating factor into the planning system. At an early date he knew that a changed situation had possibly rendered National Parks legislation unnecessary, but once convinced of the case, on expediency and other grounds, he fought consistently for an acceptable package out of what at times was a difficult set of ingredients.

After ten somewhat featureless years of Ministerial involvement, Sir Keith Joseph soon gave the impression of showing much more concern about National Parks and countryside policy. He was acutely aware of the need to set in hand new developments and he must have been disappointed not to have effected major changes in legislation.

Frederick Willey was in the fortunate position of being Minister in a new Department, untramelled by past histories and obligations, at a time when new policies were both necessary and possible. To his credit he reacted swiftly to the lessons of the Countryside in 1970 Conference and swept along with his new proposals, although these were to be considerably tempered by R. H. S. Crossman and the Ministry of Housing and Local Government.

With regard to Government Departments the importance of the Treasury can be seen throughout. The question of grant aid to local authorities for Park purposes was a sensitive one and the Treasury were keen watchdogs from the first days of the National Parks Bill. Resistance to special pleading was maintained. In the 1950s, the control over Treasury spending was particularly tight and the finan-cial stringency of this period provides an indelible stamp to the history of National Parks and Park planning at this time. The comparison with the relative liberality of the mid and late sixties is particularly striking.

The role of the Ministry of Town and Country Planning, and its successors, with regard to National Parks was ambivalent. The Department was rarely enthusiastic about the 1949 Act and regarded the Commission with no great warmth. Precise evidence is scanty, but it is difficult to resist the feeling that they considered the task of National Park and countryside planning as more properly theirs. At no time was any great imagination shown about National Parks within the Department. During the fifties and into the sixties there is no record of much innovatory thinking except when very obviously stimulated by outside sources. Silkin led at best a reluctant Ministry and Joseph could extract little enthusiasm or even willingness to respond to his own impatience.

.   .   .

Thirty years' history of National Parks provide us with insights into the formulation and execution of this one aspect of British land use and environmental planning. It is a tangled tale of compromise and expediency set against burning idealism and single minded purpose. The performance of Government comes out clearly: to legislate for community needs, to protect minority rights, to enhance the public good, to respond to change, and to balance national against local interests. In this situation we should not expect determined persuance of single objectives over a long period of time: Government is not like that, neither is land use planning. And so if the public record over National Parks fails to satisfy the purists of the amenity bodies the balance sheet of success could claim in September 1968: 5258 square miles of National Parks in England and Wales (9% of the total land area), a further 4291 square miles of Areas of Outstanding Natural Beauty (7·3%), 1273 miles of long-distance footpaths and bridleways, and 61,347 acres of access land in National Parks and Areas of Outstanding Natural Beauty.[176] In statistical terms at least this approximates to what the 1949 Act had set out to achieve.

References

CHAPTER 2

(1) Seventh Annual Report of the Ministry of Health, 1925–26, H.M.S.O., Cmd. 2724, 1926, (p. 67).
(2) Eighth Annual Report of the Ministry of Health, 1926–27, H.M.S.O., Cmd. 2938, 1927 (p. 70).
(3) Eleventh Annual Report of the Ministry of Health, 1929–30, H.M.S.O., Cmd. 3667, 1930, (p. 98).
(4) See Sixteenth Annual Report of the Ministry of Health, 1934–35, H.M.S.O., Cmd. 4978, 1935.
(5) See Eighteenth Annual Report of the Ministry of Health, 1936–37, H.M.S.O., Cmd. 5516, 1937.
(6) *Report on the Preservation of the Countryside, 1938*, Town and Country Planning Advisory Committee, Ministry of Health, H.M.S.O., 1939.
(7) Twentieth Annual Report of the Ministry of Health, 1938–39, H.M.S.O., Cmd. 6089, 1939.
(8) Fourteenth Annual Report of the Ministry of Health, 1932–33, Cmd. 4372, H.M.S.O., 1933.
(9) *Report of the National Park Committee*, Cmd. 3851, H.M.S.O., 1931.
(10) Nineteenth Annual Report of the Ministry of Health, 1937–38, Cmd. 5801, H.M.S.O., 1938.
(11) Home Office File 163094/25.
(12) Cabinet 57(38) conclusion 19.
(13) H.C. Debates, Vol. 342, 2 December 1938.
(14) Notes of meeting, Ministry of Agriculture and Fisheries, File L.U. 2914.
(15) C.P. 57(39).
(16) Ministry of Agriculture and Fisheries, File L.U. 2914.
(17) Ministry of Agriculture and Fisheries, File L.U. 2914.
(18) Ministry of Agriculture and Fisheries, File L.U. 2914.
(19) Home Office File 163094/59.
(20) Ministry of Agriculture and Fisheries, File L.U. 2913.
(21) Ministry of Agriculture and Fisheries, File L.U. 2908, letter from G. B. H. Ward to Fred Marshall, 6 May 1940.

CHAPTER 3

(22) 4 November 1941, File 95249/19, Standing Committee on National Parks of the C.P.R.E. and W., 1941–48.

(23) Minister, Meeting 8 April 1942. Committee on Reconstruction Problems, File 53/8/17.

(24) Minister, Meeting 4 May 1942, File 53/8/17.

(25) Sir William Jowitt to Lord Portal, 9 May 1942, Committee on Reconstruction Problems, File 53/8/17.

(26) Sir Kingsley Wood, Letter to Sir William Jowitt, 1 May 1942, Committee on Reconstruction Problems, File 53/1/11/2.

(27) 'Why a National Park Commission and not merely a strengthening of the planning authorities?', Standing Committee on National Parks of the C.P.R.E. and C.P.R.W., mimeo, April 1942.

(28) A. Greenwood, letter to Lord Reith, 28 October 1941, Committee on Reconstruction Problems. Investigation of Rural Industries, File 53/9/7.

(29) Lord Reith, letter to Mr. Greenwood, 29 October 1941, File 53/9/7.

(30) *Report of the Committee on Land Utilisation in Rural Areas*, Ministry of Works and Planning, H.M.S.O., Cmd. 6378, 1942.

(31) I.E.P.(43) 39 (Final), 27 August 1943, Ministry of Reconstruction File 53/1/4/18.

(32) W.P.(42) 485.

(33) File 95249/4 National Parks Preparatory Surveys.

(34) 3 October 1942. File 95249/5, Lake District National Parks, 1942–46.

(35) *National Parks in England and Wales*. Report by John Dower, Ministry of Town and Country Planning, Cmd. 6628, H.M.S.O., 1945.

(36) *The Control of Land Use*, Cmd. 6537, H.M.S.O., 1944.

(37) File 95249/5, Lake District National Parks, 1942–46. This file is the source material for these paragraphs dealing with the Lake District.

(38) M.H.L.G. File 95249/16A2.

(39) September 1944, Treasury File S.S. 398/01 Part A, National Parks and Access to the Countryside Bill.

(40) S.S. 398/01 Part A, *op. cit.*

(41) 12 December 1944, File S.S. 398/01 Part A, *op. cit.*

(42) H.C. Debates, Vol. 403, Col. 2381, 18 October 1944.

(43) R.(45) 44.

(44) R.(45) 49.

(45) 4 May 1945, File S.S. 398/01 Part A, *op. cit.*

(46) File 95249E/1/Part I. National Parks Committee.

(47) L.P.(45) 136, 14 August 1945.

(48) File 95249/D/10/2 Part I. Evidence to National Parks Committee. Where not otherwise stated, this file is the source for this section of the chapter.

(49) File 95249E/1/Part III. National Parks Committee, Meetings of Main Committee. Thirteenth meeting, 14–15 August 1946.

(50) *Report of the National Parks Committee (England and Wales)*, Cmd. 7121, 1947.

(51) National Parks Committee, Meetings of Main Committee. Fourteenth meeting, 12–13 September 1946.

(52) *op. cit.* Fifth meeting, 15–16 January 1946.

(53) *op. cit.* Fourth meeting, 4–5 December 1945.
(54) *op. cit.* Sixth meeting, 31 January–1 February 1946.
(55) *op. cit.* Thirteenth meeting, 14–15 August 1946.
(56) *op. cit.* Eighth meeting, 20–21 March 1946.
(57) *Footpaths and Access to the Countryside: Report of the Special Committee (England and Wales)*, Cmd. 7207, 1947.
(58) *op. cit.* Seventh meeting, 19–20 February 1946.
(59) File 95249/D/14.

CHAPTER 4

(60) 16 August 1941. Department of Agriculture for Scotland File 107088 I/1.
(61) Letter, 5 October 1942. File 107088 I/1.
(62) Department of Agriculture for Scotland File 107088/1/N.
(63) M.T.C.P. File 95249/17.
(64) Department of Agriculture for Scotland File 107088/R.
(65) Letter, 27 January 1943, File 95249/17.
(66) Letter, 27 October 1943, File 107088/R.
(67) File P/NP/5/1/1. Minutes of evidence.
(68) R.(45) 49, 7 May 1945.
(69) Department of Health for Scotland File P/NP/5/3/4/2.
(70) *National Parks and the Conservation of Nature in Scotland*, Report by the Scottish National Parks Committee and the Scottish Wild Life Committee, Department of Health for Scotland, Cmd. 7235, H.M.S.O., 1947.
(71) File P/NP/5/3/3.

CHAPTER 5

(72) Secretary's Bill Papers Volume 259G, 12 February 1947.
(73) Volume 259G. Sir Thomas Sheepshanks to Henderson, 6 April 1948.
(74) E. S. Hill to Secretary M.T.C.P., 27 November 1947. File 95249/35/2.
(75) Sir Thomas Sheepshanks to Minister, 22 April 1948, Volume 259G.
(76) Treasury File S.S. 398/05.
(77) Treasury File 398/01 Part C.
(78) 9 June 1948, Treasury File 398/01 Part C.
(79) 11 June 1948, Volume 259G.
(80) Treasury File 398/01 Part C.
(81) Volume 259G.
(82) Volume 259G.
(83) 21 May 1948, Volume 259G.
(84) 22 November 1948, Volume 259G.
(85) 27 October 1947, File 95249/35/2.
(86) File 95249/35/2.
(87) Volume 259G.
(88) Internal note, Winifred M. Fox to E. S. Hill, 19 March 1948, File 95249/35/2.

(89) Volume 259G.
(90) Sir Thomas Sheepshanks to E. S. Hill, 10 March 1948, Volume 259G.
(91) Volume 259G.
(92) Note from Sir Thomas Sheepshanks to Minister, 20 April 1948, Volume 259G.
(93) Letter from E. A. Sharp to Gatliff, 30 April 1948, Volume 259G.
(94) L.P.(48) 33, 23 April 1948.
(95) E. A. Sharp to Gatliff, 30 April 1948, Volume 259G.
(96) L.P.(48) 54, 2 July 1948.
(97) L.P.(49) 8, 4 February 1949.
(98) Sir Bernard Gilbert to Sir Thomas Sheepshanks, 21 January 1949, Treasury File 398/01 Part D.
(99) L.P.(49) 9, 4 February 1949.
(100) Fraser (Treasury) to Reynolds (M.T.C.P.), 21 February 1949, Treasury File 398/01 Part D.
(101) Sir Thomas Sheepshanks to Sir Bernard Gilbert, 28 February 1949, Treasury File 398/01 Part D.
(102) H.P.C.(49) 10th meeting, 15 March 1949.
(103) Fraser to Sir H. Brittain, February 1949, Treasury File 398/01 Part D.
(104) Visit by Sir Thomas Sheepshanks and Deputy Secretary to Sir Bernard Gilbert, 17 February 1949, Volume 259G.
(105) H.C. Debates, Vol. 464, Cols 1469–1470, 31 March 1949.
(106) H.C. Debates, Vol. 464, Col. 1493, 31 March 1949.
(107) 26 July 1949. Volume 259G.

CHAPTER 6

(108) M.H.L.G. File 95295/15.
(109) M.H.L.G. File 95295/17.
(110) M.H.L.G. File 95295/17.
(111) M.H.L.G. File 95295/17.
(112) M.H.L.G. File 95295/16.
(113) Fifth Report, National Parks Commission, H.M.S.O., 1954.
(114) M.H.L.G. File C2/DH/4.
(115) M.H.L.G. File 91808/2/21.
(116) Eighth Report, National Parks Commission, H.M.S.O., 1958.
(117) Ninth Report, National Parks Commission, H.M.S.O., 1958.
(118) Eleventh Report, National Parks Commission, H.M.S.O., 1960.
(119) Eleventh Report, National Parks Commission, H.M.S.O., 1960.
(120) Third Report, National Parks Commission, H.M.S.O., 1952.
(121) *Report of the Royal Commission on Common Land, 1958, Cmnd. 462.*
(122) H.A.(58) 152.
(123) H.A.(58) 24th Meeting.
(124) M.H.L.G. File 91808/1/8/1. Brief for Parliamentary Secretary, Blenkinsop's Bill, Legislation Committee, 26 January 1959.

CHAPTER 7

(125) M.H.L.G. File C2/155/1/A.
(126) M.H.L.G. File C2/DH/4.
(127) 23 March 1961. M.H.L.G. File PC2/161/1 Part B.
(128) M.H.L.G. File PC2/161/1 Part B.
(129) M.H.L.G. File PC2/161/1 Part C.
(130) M.H.L.G., Departmental note, 'Amendment of the National Park and Access to the Countryside Act, 1949', P9, 12 December 1962. M.H.L.G. File C2/155/1 Part B.
(131) H.C. Debates, Vol. 668, Cols 811–901, 30 November 1962.
(132) M.H.L.G. File C2/155/1/C.
(133) M.H.L.G. File C2/155/1/B.
(134) M.H.L.G. File C2/155/1/C.
(135) Fourteenth Report, National Parks Commission, H.M.S.O., 1963.
(136) M.H.L.G. File C2/155/1/C.
(137) M.H.L.G. File C2/155/1/C.
(138) 19 December 1963, revised 22 January 1974, M.H.L.G. File PG/475/1.
(139) *The Countryside in 1970: a study conference*, H.M.S.O., 1964.
(140) M.H.L.G. File P9/475/1.
(141) 'The exploding need for recreational space: Minister's thoughts on best use of countryside', M.H.L.G., 12 May 1964.
(142) 6 October 1964. M.H.L.G. File P9/475/1.
(143) 'Leisure and Countryside Amenity: a fresh appraisal by the National Parks Commission', N.P.C., 28 March 1965. M.H.L.G. File PC2/475/2.
(144) Sixteenth Report, National Parks Commission, H.M.S.O., 1965.
(145) Use of the Countryside for Recreation', Note by the Ministry of Land and Natural Resources, 1 June 1965.
(146) M.H.L.G. File PG1/475/1.
(147) 'Use of the Countryside for Recreation', H.(65) 74, 20 July 1965.
(148) H.(65) 79, 21 July 1965.
(149) H.(65) 82, 23 July 1965.
(150) 'Use of the Countryside for Recreation', H.(65) 103, 6 October 1965.
(151) *Leisure in the Countryside, England and Wales*, Cmnd. 2928, H.M.S.O., 1966.
(152) M.H.L.G. File B/31/14/3 Part C.
(153) M.H.L.G. File PC2/611/11.
(154) M.H.L.G. File B/31/2/2.
(155) M.H.L.G. File B/31/14/4/A.

CHAPTER 8

(156) L.P.(48) 36, 20 April 1948.
(157) Department of Health for Scotland File P/NP/1/1. (National Parks Proposed Legislation 1947–48).

(158) Department of Agriculture for Scotland File 107088/NPC/A. Post War Reconstruction—Scottish National Parks Committee—Proposed National Park at Loch Lomond, Trossachs.

(159) Scottish Development Department, File P/NP/1/2. Proposed Scottish National Parks and Access Legislation, 1950.

(160) File P/NP/2/1/4. Department of Health for Scotland. National Parks: Report by Scottish Council for National Parks.

(161) Scottish Development Department File P/NP/1/6.

(162) H.A.(60) 97, 13 July 1960.

(163) H.A.(60) 16th Meeting, 19 July 1960.

(164) L.C.(61) 13th Meeting, 25 April 1961. Considered Memorandum by Secretary of State for Scotland on the Countryside (Scotland) Bill, L.C.(61) 44.

(165) H.A.(63) 12th Meeting, 28 June 1963.

(166) Scottish Development Department File P/NP/A National Parks General.

(167) Scottish Development Department File P/NP/A National Parks General.

(168) M.H.L.G. File PG1/175/1.

(169) H.P.(64) 5th Meeting, 14 February 1964.

(170) Scottish Development Department File NP/1/6/3.

(171) *The Countryside in 1970. Countryside: Planning and Development in Scotland*, Report of Study Group Nine to Second Countryside Conference, 10–12 November 1965.

(172) H.(66) 76, 10 October 1966.

(173) H.(66) 21st Meeting, 14 October 1966.

(174) C.C.(66) 13. Minute 3.

CHAPTER 9

(175) *Report of the National Parks Policies Review Committee*, H.M.S.O., 1974.

(176) Nineteenth Report of the National Parks Commission and First Report of the Countryside Commission, H.M.S.O., 1968.

Abbreviations

C.C.   Cabinet Conclusions.
C.P.   Cabinet Papers.
H.   Home Affairs Committee.
H.A.   Home Affairs Committee.
H.P.   Home Affairs Committee.
H.P.C. Legislation Committee.
I.E.P. Official Committee on Post War Internal Economic Problems.
L.C.   Legislation Committee.
L.P.   Lord President's Committee.
R.   Reconstruction Committee.
W.P.   War Cabinet Papers.

INDEX